The Place of Religion in the Liberal Philosophy of Constant, Tocqueville, and Lord Acton

The Place of Religion in the Liberal Philosophy of Constant, Tocqueville, and Lord Acton

A Dissertation Submitted to the University of Chicago's
Faculty of the Division of the Social Sciences
in Candidacy for the Degree of Doctor of Philosophy
for the Committee on Social Thought,
Chaired by F. A. Hayek

By
Ralph Raico

Ludwig von Mises Institute
AUBURN, ALABAMA

Ludwig von Mises Institute
518 West Magnolia Avenue
Auburn, Alabama 36832

Ph: (334) 844-2500
Fax: (334) 844-2583

mises.org

10 9 8 7 6 5 4 3 2 1

ISBN: 978-1-61016-000-1

Contents

Introduction

Religion and liberty—few issues are more controversial among current-day libertarians. At least four positions can be distinguished. One well-known position holds that religion and liberty are separate spheres that are almost hermetically sealed from one another, while any historical point of contact is purely accidental or contingent. According to another wide-spread position, religion and liberty are outright antagonistic. These advocates see in religion the most deadly foe of individual liberty, an even greater enemy of mankind than the state. A third position contends that religion and liberty are complementary: on the one hand, pious men facilitate the workings of a society with minimal or no government and, on the other hand, political liberty facilitates religious life as each one sees fit. Finally, some thinkers defend a fourth position, namely, that religion—and in particular the Christian faith—is fundamental for individual liberty, both as far as the historical record is concerned and on the conceptual level.

In our thoroughly secularised culture, the third position is held to be daring and the fourth insolent. Yet today, I do believe that they are both true and that the third is a skin-deep statement of the truth, while the fourth goes to the root of the matter. Once a pagan interventionist, I first saw the truths of libertarian political theory, and eventually I started to realize that the light of these truths was but a reflection of the encompassing and eternal light that radiates from God through His Son and the Holy Spirit. This realisation has been a slow process and I could not say now when and where it will end. But I can pinpoint the circumstances of its beginnings. I can pinpoint the one writer who got this stone in me rolling.

At the beginning of my academic career I had the good fortune and privilege to translate Ralph Raico's magnificent essay on the history of

German liberalism into my mother tongue.[1] This book brilliantly displays the virtues of its author: his scholarship, his wittiness, his righteousness, and his courage. For me it was an eye-opener. It set the record straight on the main protagonists. In particular, Friedrich Naumann, a man of undeserved libertarian fame, was thrown out of the pantheon of the champions of liberty, while Eugen Richter, today virtually unknown, was elevated to his rightful place as the foremost leader of the *fin-de-siècle* German party of liberty. Ralph Raico explained that the German liberals failed, not least of all, because at some point they started missing their target. Rather than opposing the state, they began to see the enemy in organised religion. They endorsed Bismarck's repressive laws designed to wage a culture war on the Catholic Church.

A typical case in point was Rudolf Virchow, a surgeon, professor, and liberal party leader, who displayed the very same haughty and ignorant attitude toward organised religion that is also the intellectual plague of modern culture, and of modern libertarianism in particular. Ralph Raico's book highlighted the lines of continuity between the Virchows of all times and the French Enlightenment. The thoroughly anti-clerical writings of Voltaire, Rousseau, Didérot, d'Alembert, Helvétius, and so many other apparent champions of individual liberty and opponents of oppression had created a continental European culture of liberalism in which the antagonism of faith and freedom was taken for granted. As a consequence, religious people have always been suspicious of this movement. It seemed as though one had to choose between religion and liberty.

However, Professor Raico also stressed that there was another tradition within classical liberal thought, one that recognised the interdependence between religion and liberty. This tradition includes most notably the three great thinkers that Professor Raico has portrayed in his 1970 doctoral dissertation, which explains how the political thought of Benjamin Constant, Alexis de Tocqueville, and Lord Acton flowed from their religious convictions. This early work is here reprinted and made available for all people of good will. At the beginning of the twenty-first century, it has not lost its timeliness and importance as a tool for re-understanding the history of liberalism. I salute its publication and predict it will open many more eyes.

Jörg Guido Hülsmann
Angers, France
June 2010

[1] See Ralph Raico, *Die Partei der Freiheit. Studien zur Geschichte des deutschen Liberalismus* (Stuttgart: Lucius & Lucius, 1999).

CHAPTER 1

Benjamin Constant

"He loved liberty as other men love power" was the judgment passed on Benjamin Constant by a nineteenth-century admirer. Constant's great public concern, all throughout his adult life, was the attainment of a free society, especially for his adopted country, France. And if a by no means uncritical French commentator exaggerated in calling him the inventor of liberalism,[1] it is nevertheless true that in the second and third decades of the last century, when liberalism was the spectre haunting Europe, Constant shared with Jeremy Bentham the honor of being the chief theoretical champion of the creed. His influence—particularly because his involvement in French politics under the Restoration regime gave him a platform in the most attentively watched legislature on the continent—was widespread; he had important groups of followers in France, Italy, and south Germany, and disciples as far away as Russia.[2]

The comparison of Constant with Bentham is one worth making in detail, although this will not be attempted here. While each can be taken as representative of one of the great streams of early nineteenth-century liberal thought, their differences were almost as significant as their similarities.

[1] Émile Faguet, *Politiques et moralistes du XIXe siècle, première série* (Paris: Boiven, 1891), p. 255.

[2] William Holdheim, *Benjamin Constant* (New York: Hillary, 1961), p. 73.

Bentham and his disciples refined the rationalist and utilitarian position of most of eighteenth-century French liberalism; Constant, on the other hand, occupied himself with breaking through this mold and attaching liberalism to the romantic and historic thought emerging into prominence in his day, especially in Germany. Associated with this is his effort, which was to be repeated in differing forms by Tocqueville and Acton, to end the centuries-old hostility between Christianity and liberal thought, and to turn religious faith to the advantage of the free society, now confronting new and peculiarly dangerous enemies. It is this endeavor on the part of these three writers which will comprise the substance of this paper.

While we may pass over Constant's generally erratic upbringing and the complex romantic life which has constituted the bulk of most biographies of him, this does not imply that his personal experiences were irrelevant to his political and social thought.[3] One phase of his biography in particular is of prime importance in understanding his thought and cannot be avoided: that is the fact that Constant began thinking on social problems under the sway of the ideas of the French Enlightenment, and that a good deal of his intellectual career consists of the struggle to free himself from this mental framework. Of key importance in the formation of his earlier views were his participation in the salon of Madame Suard, where he came into contact with La Harpe, Marmontel and other remnants of the pre-Revolutionary philosophical demimonde; his liaison with Madame de Charriere, herself a perfect Encyclopedist *femme d'esprit* in thought and sensibility;[4] and his association with Talleyrand, Abbé Sieyès and others in the Cercle Constitutionnel, where he quickly became a young

[3]A recent interpreter has correctly stated of Constant: "Vièle seiner Ideen lassen sich ganz überhaupt nur verstehen aus seiner Biographie, aus den Einsichten, die er auf.seinem eigenene Lebensweg empfing." Lothar Gall, *Benjamin Constant; Seine Politische Ideenwelt und der deutsche Vormärz* (Wiesbaden: Steiner, 1963), pp. 1–2. Cf., Faguet, op. cit., pp. 212–213.

[4]Of Madame de Charrière, Constant himself relates (in *Adolphe*): "J'avais contracté dans mes conversations avec la femme qui la première avait développé mes idées, une insurmontable aversion pour toutes les maximes communes, et pour toutes les formules dogmatiques." *Œuvres*, ed. by Alfred Roulin (Paris: Pléiade, 1957), p. 50. It was during a sojourn at her home that Constant first conceived and outlined his project for a great work on religion. Holdheim calls her, as Constant depicts her in the *Cahier Rouge*, "almost a symbol of the Age of Reason" and "the very personification of the hero's great temptation to dissolve all the apparent solidity of the surrounding world in the test tube of the critical intellect." Ibid., pp. 34–35.

star and was made secretary.[5] Thus, Constant commenced his intellectual career endowed with a store of conceptions and preconceptions on the great issues of social and political theory, especially on religion, ethics and the place of the individual in society. In the words of Saltet, the influence which "le marque définitivement de son empreinte fut celle du XVIIIe siècle. Du XVIIIe siècle il a l'immoralité naïve, les moeurs dépavées, la corruption raffinée et élégante, et ce cynisme dont aucune autre époque n'a donné l'exemple ... Du XVIIIe siècle il eut sans doute aussi l'irréligion."[6]

As time went on, Constant battled with this heritage, but he was never able to shrug it off completely. As we shall see, his personal problems with religious faith may be taken as typical of his relationship with the ideas of the eighteenth century: after a good deal of struggle, he was able to come to a position discernibly different from that of the Enlightenment; nevertheless, the marks of the first world outlook he had accepted remained with him to the end.

The influences that contributed to diluting his earlier rationalism were those emanating from his close association with Madame de Staël; his interest and involvement in the German intellectual world of his time (especially his interest in the thought of Harder and Schleiermacher); and his own personal needs.[7]

This last deserves explanation. Constant, after awhile, began in a manner reminiscent of Jean-Jacques Rousseau, to link the eighteenth century with a whole style of life which excluded any authentic feeling and crushed all nobler sentiment by means of a shallow brilliance and wit. As early as 1805 he says of Voltaire's *La Pucelle*:

> C'est bien l'ouvrage d'un siècle qui a appris à se moquer de lui-même comme des autres, de ses opinions comme des opinions opposées ; c'est une sorte de titillation d'esprit, résultat d'un grand épuisement et l'irritabilité qui accompagne un extrême épuisement.[8]

---

[5] Eugene Asse, "Benjamin Constant et le Directoire," *Revue de la Révolution* 16 (August 1889), p. 437.

[6] Mathieu Saltet, *Benjamin Constant : Historien de la Religion* (Geneva: Société Général d'Imprimerie, 1905), p. 15.

[7] Gall, op. cit., p. 22; Saltet, op. cit., p. 27.

[8] In the *Journaux Intimes*, in Benjamin Constant, *Œuvres*, ed. by Alfred Roulin (Paris : Pléiade, 1957), p. 479.

At times he raises this into an element of the French national character: "Principe français, qu'il faut juger la plaisanterie indépendamment de son objet, c'est-à-dire qu'il est égal qu'elle soit dirigée contre la vertu ou contre le crime."[9] At other times, Constant's indictment of the "nihilism" of the eighteenth century reaches extreme depths of intensity and bitterness. He attributes to it a pathological, death-dealing quality. The following passage, for instance, recalls de Maistre:

> Étrange philosophie que celle du XVIIIe siècle, se jouant d'elle-même et des autres, prenant à tâche de discréditer non seulement les préjugés reçus, non seulement les idées consolantes et morales—qu'on aurait pu séparer de ces préjugés,—mais se moquant de ses propres principes, trouvant du plaisir à ne rien laisser qui soit exempt de ridicule, à tout dégrader, à tout avilir.[10]

Here, again, we find Constant's characteristic insistence on the strange decadence of the Enlightenment, at least in its final phase, when it was apparently propelled by a will to destruction so complete as to finally consume even its own principles and itself. Constant confesses that he felt himself "frappé de terreur" when reading Holbach's *Système de la nature*: "Ce long acharnement d'un vieillard à fermer devant lui tout avenir, cette inexplicable soif de la destruction ... me paraissaient un bizarre délire ... [Holbach] me présentait avec triomphe le néant comme terme de moi-même et des objets de mes affections."[11] In warring on this element of the spirit of the eighteenth century, Constant conceived of himself as combating a sort of intellectualist madness, which had proved itself to be disastrous for the moral life of France and, as we shall see, a great danger for European society in the future. But beyond that, it is of the utmost importance that Constant could not simply view the prevalence of this mode of thought in a detached manner, for he considered that he himself was cursed by it. The inability to feel emotions, or to be certain that one is authentically feeling them, was a characteristic he attributed to himself. Partly, it came from his family background;[12] but partly also, there is little doubt, he felt that it was

[9] Ibid., p. 476.

[10] Quoted in Saltet, op. cit., pp. 31–32. Constant adds: "Quand on lit avec attention les ouvages de cette époque, on n'estétonné ni de ce qui a suivi, ni de ce qui en résulte à présent."

[11] *De la religion considérée dans sa source, ses formes, et ses développements* (Paris: Leroux, 1924), vol. 1, p. 11.

[12] Gall, op. cit., p. 5.

reinforced and exaggerated by the times and society in which he lived. He was, over much of his life, in the unfortunate position of one who desires to desire. He felt that a too early and too thorough "sophistication" had robbed him of the possibility, and on one occasion he bursts out: "Revenez donc, passion que j'ai amorties, plaisirs simples et doux que j'ai repoussés, vertus obscures et journalières que je me suis fait un mérite de mépriser; sentiments d'amour, d'amitié, de bienveillance, heureuse crédulité qu'on m'a arrachée pour de précoces et fastueuses leçons, revenez!"[13] The deep hostility on his part to many aspects of Enlightenment thought and sensibility, which we will observe again and again, is ultimately rooted in this preoccupation with his own complex problems. The fact that his psyche in this way mirrors cultural currents of great historical significance is surely one of the sources of the fascination it has exerted on French and other critics.

Constant's lifelong public concern was, as has been indicated, the founding and maintenance of a liberal social and political order. This has misled a number of commentators into supposing that his sole end was "negative," merely the emancipation of the individual from the bonds of political authority and, to a lesser extent, of tradition. Henri Michel, for instance, remarks that "Benjamin Constant a mérité le même reproche [as Édouard Laboulaye] pour ... n'avoir vu dans l'individualisme qu'une sauvegarde contre l'abus de l'autorité."[14] Alfred Fabre-Luce goes so far as to state that Constant's later marked sympathy for religion can be explained simply by the fact that he came to see it as a support for freedom, rather than, as had previously been the case, for authority.[15] Both these writers ignore the clearly stated position of Constant, which is that there exists a higher moral goal than freedom itself and that freedom is best regarded as a means for the attainment of that goal. Of organized social life in general, Constant says, "Toutes les institutions sociales ne sont que des formes adoptées pour le même but, pour le plus grand perfectionnement de l'espèce humaine."[16] The high value attached to liberty is due to the fact that it is an aid in this

[13] Ibid.

[14] Henri Michel, *L'Idée de l'état* (Paris: Hachette, 1896), p. 315.

[15] Alfred Fabre-Luce, *Benjamin Constant* (Paris: Fayard, 1939), pp. 202–203.

[16] *Œuvres*, p. 1610.

evolution. "La liberté n'est d'un prix inestimable que parce qu'elle donne à notre esprit de la justesse ; à notre caractère, de la force ; à notre âme de l'élévation."[17] Sometimes he states the connection between liberty and the true end of man in terms suggestive of the romanticism prevalent in his day:

> Le combat que se livrent en lui [i.e., in the individual] le bien et le mal, ses tâtonnements, ses tentatives infructueuses, ses erreurs, et jusqu'à ses crimes ... [c]es choses sont une portion de la lute qui est son partage, et cette lute est son moyen de perfectionnement.[18]

It is only through a trial and error process, then, that man can come across the best answers to the problems confronting him, and more importantly, forge himself into a virtuous and effective individual. It is useless to hope for the realization of these ends through authority. Constant allies himself here with his friend, Wilhelm von Humboldt, in equating coerced behavior with mechanical nonhuman activity and contrasting it with the freedom and spontaneity characteristic of truly human action:

> Conduit vers ce but par on pouvoir qui asservirait sa volonté, il perdrait la qualité d'être libre ; et réduit au rang de machine, sa perfection ne serait plus que du mécanisme. L'amélioration n'aurait plus rien de moral.[19]

The perfectioning of man can come about only through "ses propres efforts, par l'exercice de ses facultés, par l'énergie de son libre arbitre."[20]

Besides the value of liberty as the indispensable means for the attainment of the chief end of man, the moral perfectioning of the individual, there were other ends which liberty served, in Constant's view. Probably the most important of these was the part it played in cultural evolution.

---

[17] Ibid., p. 1054.

[18] *De la religion*, vol. 2, pp. 212–213.

[19] Ibid., p. 213.

[20] Ibid., p. 212. It is interesting to note that Constant claimed for his approach the merit of being able to solve the traditional central problem of theodicy. Of the problem of evil he states, "si nous concevons l'être suprême comme ayant marqué pour but à sa créature, non le bonheur, mais l'amélioration, tout s'explique. Un nouvel horizon se découvre. Nous nous élevons à une hauteur nouvelle. Le bonheur et le malheur ne sont que des moyens : Dieu n'est point injuste en les employant. Toute autre solution de l'existence du mal est insuffisante, et ne repose que sur des sophismes." *De la religion*, vol. 4, pp. 142–143, n.

Here Constant's ideas show most clearly the influence of non-French—principally German and Scottish—models; this is one of the ways, too, in which his thought diverges most from the customary cut-and-dried path of utilitarian liberal thinking.

Constant himself attributes the core of the idea to the Germans:

> Les Allemands ont le grand mérite ... de reconnaître presque tous une vérité fondamentale ... c'est que tout est progressif dans l'homme. Aucune de ses notions ne reste au même point ; elles se développent malgré les résistances, se font jour à travers les obstacles ; et, à la fin de chaque espace de temps un peu long, elles se trouvent avoir subi des modifications, reçu des améliorations essentielles ... [This holds true for] les formes sociales, politiques, religieuses.[21]

One of the implications of this doctrine of the progressive evolution of social forms is that the human intellect itself is subject to historical evolution: as Constant puts it, "le développement de l'intelligence n'est lui-même que le résultat de la société."[22] Thus, the attention of political and social theory is shifted to the conditions for optimal social development.

This development, while progressive, must be understood as a very slow and gradual one. Constant expressed his differences from his friend, Charles de Villers, in this regard: "[C]omme il croit à l'influence des livres et à la possibilité d'améliorer les hommes ! Moi aussi je crois à la perfectibilité, mais ce n'est pas si individuellement. Les siècles l'amènent, mais chaque homme en particulier n'y contribue que d'une manière imperceptible."[23] It is not individual Great Leaders, Great Teachers, Great Books, or anything of the kind that is responsible for advancement along the road to human perfection. Rather, the mechanism of social progress is to be sought in much broader and more profound social forces.

The basic conception of historical evolution which Constant holds is an idealistic one (as he puts it, an "idéalisme tel que je le conçois"). There exist, in each historical epoch, certain "idées," the totality of which constitutes the spirit of the times. In every area of social life these ideas move toward their fulfillment and realization. In striving towards this end, however, they run up against established institutions. Such institutions

[21] Ibid., vol. 1, pp. 124–125.

[22] Ibid., p. 154.

[23] *Œuvres*, p. 454.

had at one time served important functions: they answered human needs according to the best knowledge available at the time; they were, in fact, the result of the ideas of their own epoch. But new times had produced new needs and new knowledge embodied in the new ideas. A struggle therefore ensues, in which the antiquated institutions are gradually eroded and finally crumble. Institutions more appropriate to the changed spirits of the time then take their place. Then the process is repeated. As he states in *De l'esprit de conquête*:

> Au moment où certaines institutions se sont établies, comme elles étaient proportionnées à l'état des lumières et des mœurs, elles avaient une utilité, une bonté relative. A mesure que l'esprit humain a fait des progrès, ces avantages ont diminué ; les institutions se sont modifiées. Vouloir rétablir ces institutions dans ce qu'on nomma leur pureté primitive, serait alors une grande faute ; car cette pureté se trouverait précisément la chose la plus opposée aux idées contemporaines, et la plus propre à faire du mal.[24]

It will be seen that what Constant is positing here is a dialectical process, whereby the growth of enlightenment produces a state of the "social mind" different from that which had given rise to the present social institutions. This incompatibility results in strains in the existing social structure; in response, the social institutions begin to be modified.

Whether the change will be a peaceful or a revolutionary one depends on how the constituted social authorities treat the incipient change. The correct attitude is one of complete laissez-faire, avoiding the attempts both to preserve obsolete institutions and to substitute more theoretically perfect ones for those which naturally develop:

> Le mal n'est jamais dans ce qui existe naturellement, mais dans ce qu'on prolonge ou dans ce qu'on rétablit par la ruse ou la force. Le véritable bien, c'est la proportion. La nature la maintient toujours quand on laisse la nature libre. Toute disproportion est pernicieuse. Ce qui est usé, ce qui est hâtif est également funeste.[25]

It is on this social theory that Constant will take his stand and from which he will launch his condemnations both of the theocratic reactionaries of his own time and the Jacobin revolutionaries of few years before: "c'est

[24] Ibid., p. 1613.

[25] *De la religion*, vol. 1, p. 363.

la même erreur, différement appliquée. Ce sont toujours les droits de l'opinion qu 'on dispute ; les uns ne veulent pas l'atteindre ; les autres ne veulent pas marcher avec elle."[26] Constant's advice on these questions is simple, even platitudinous sounding, but rests, as I have indicated, on a suggestive attempt at a general social theory:

> restez fidèles à la justice, qui est de toutes les époques ; respectez la liberté, qui prépare tous les biens ; consentez à ce que beaucoup de choses se développent sans vous, et confiez au passé sa propre défense, à l'avenir son propre accomplissement.[27]

What Constant conceived more specifically to be the mechanism whereby progress occurs in social institutions may be gathered from his attitude on the standardization of weights and measures, the introduction of the metric system, and other such reforms of the Revolution:

> Si l'autorité peut, sans porter atteinte à la propriété particulière et aux droits individuels, ouvrir un chemin direct, elle fait bien. Mais qu'elle se borne à ouvrir un chemin ... tôt ou tard l'intérêt sera vainqueur, et le changement que l'on désire, moins chèrement acheté, sera plus complet et plus irrévocable.[28]

This is about as much of a lead as Constant affords us as to how, under a regime of laissez-faire, the ideas are supposed to modify received institutions gradually and peacefully. Nonetheless, his view that only such a regime will allow for the satisfactory fitting of the established social order to the ever progressive spirit of the age is unambiguous.

❧

In a sense, however, the interpretation of Constant which makes liberty his ultimate goal, if mistaken, is understandable: his position in the history of political thought is, above all, that of a sophisticated, post-Revolutionary liberal. He was for years almost the personification of the liberal movement in France. As he wrote of himself, in the last years of his life:

---

[26] *Œuvres*, pp. 1612–1613.
[27] Ibid., p. 1614.
[28] Ibid., p. 1610.

> J'ai défendu quarante ans le même principe, liberté en tout, en religion, en philosophie, en littérature, en industrie, en politique : et par liberté, j'entends le triomphe de l'individualité, tant sur l'autorité qui voudrait gouverner par le despotisme, que sur les masses qui réclament le droit d'asservir la minorité à la majorité.[29]

Thus, while the development of human personality and the realization of the possibility of moral choice are the ultimate ends served by liberty, within the political realm, freedom assumes the status of an ultimate end and the value of highest priority; for, as he asserted in a letter to his uncle: "Je crois que ce qu'il faut aux hommes pour arriver à la perfection dans tout ce qui les intéresse, c'est la liberté, par conséquent l'absence de toute autorité exercitive."[30] Wholly characteristic of the importance Constant attached to individual freedom is a statement such as the following: "sur elle [liberty] s'appuie la morale publique et privée, sur elle reposent les calculs de l'industrie. Sans elle il n'y a pour les hommes ni paix, ni dignité, ni bonheur."[31]

As against his contemporary Bentham, however, Constant believed liberty to consist in the realization of the rights of man.[32] There is nothing particularly original in Constant's doctrine of rights, a judgment that holds also for a good deal of the rest of his strictly political thought: much of it is a repetition of what were well-known liberal principles (although, of course, not always adhered to) in France for perhaps three generations by Constant's time.

What Constant emphasized, in distinction to certain liberals of the pre-Revolutionary period, was that government was a collection of standing threats to individual freedom: it was, he proclaimed, the "natural enemy of liberty"; governments will always look on war as "a means of increasing their authority"; ministers, of whatever party, are by nature "the eternal adversaries of freedom of the press."[33] Thus, with Constant, the

---

[29] Ibid., p. 835.

[30] Quoted in Gall, op. cit., p. 151.

[31] Quoted ibid., p. 303.

[32] Michel's remark that "tandis que Rousseau ... proclame les droits de *l'homme*, Benjamin Constant se borne à proclamer ceux *du citoyen Français*," is incomprehensible, given Constant's reiteration of his belief in natural rights. Michel, op. cit., p. 303. (Italics in original.)

[33] *Cours de politique constitutionnelle*, ed. by Édouard Laboulaye (Paris: Guillaume, 1872), vol. 1, pp. xix–xx.

chief articulator of his generation's liberal ideals, we see the clear emergence of classical liberalism's "state hatred," which, after the eighteenth century's ambiguous attitude, marks its theory to the present day.[34]

At the base of this suspicion of government is a marked skepticism concerning human nature when it disposes of great power. As he remarks on one occasion: "Chacun, pour juger du mal qu'occasionne le caprice sans bornes et le pouvoir sans frein, n'a qu'à descendre dans son propre Cœur."[35] On this subject his model was Montesquieu, for whom he had a boundless admiration.[36] Constant's posture of deep distrust towards the wielders of political power echoes the famous judgment of the eighteenth-century writer: "c'est une expérience éternelle que tout homme qui a du pouvoir est porté à en abuser ; il va jusqu'à ce qu'il trouve des limites." Moreover, his remedy for this problem is likewise in the tradition that Montesquieu represented when he added: "Pour qu'on ne puisse abuser du pouvoir, il faut que, par la disposition des choses, le pouvoir arrête le pouvoir."[37]

The system of checks and balances was in Constant's thought, to operate at many different points in the governmental structure, and the general outlines are familiar enough. There was to be a bicameral legislature, including a House of Peers to be selected independently of democratic opinion (a demand of the Anglophiles in the National Assembly of 1789, whom Constant admires). Constant further divided power between the legislature and the judiciary, which was to consist of judges whose immovability from office was guaranteed. An additional limit on the power of the central government was implied in a system of departmental and municipal rights. The special place of the king in Constant's conception, the "pouvoir neutre," also contributed to this ultimate end.[38]

In addition to the guarantee of individual rights built into the system of government itself, Constant looked to certain social institutions to provide further guarantees. One of the most important of these was the press.

---

[34] Michel, op. cit., p. 309.

[35] *De la religion*, vol. 3, pp. 343–335.

[36] Cf., for instance, his comment in the *Journaux Intimes* (1804): "Tout ce qu'il a dit, jusque dans les plus petites choses, se vérifie tous les jours." *Œuvres*, p. 261.

[37] Baron Charles Secondat de Montesquieu, *De l'esprit des lois* (Paris: Garnier, 1961), bk. 11, chap. 4.

[38] Georges de Lauris, *Benjamin Constant et les droits individuels* (Paris: Rousseau, 1903), passim.

Freedom of the press, in this way, took on the double character: it was itself a precious right, and it acted as one of the most powerful extra-governmental guarantees of all rights as well. The function of the press as a tribune for those whose rights were violated was incessantly emphasized by Constant. During his career as deputy in the French legislature, he tirelessly fought all the various expedients which the government devised to interfere with this freedom, and was considered the liberals' parliamentary expert on the subject.[39]

But Constant's originality begins to emerge in his looking beyond these traditional guarantees to other social institutions and forces. It is here that he grapples with one of the fundamental problems of nineteenth-century liberal, and particularly French liberal, thought. The Revolutionary period had witnessed constant experimentation with constitutional arrangements. Able political minds—Sieyès is merely the foremost example—devoted a large part of their energy to the construction of basically liberal state edifices; and it had all ended in a situation where the combined military forces of all the other powers were necessary to prise a military dictatorship from the reins of government in France. As Constant put it:

> Toutes les constitutions qui ont été données à la France garantissaient également la liberté individuelle, et, sous l'empire de ces constitutions, la liberté individuelle a été violée sans cesse. C'est qu'une simple déclaration ne suffit pas.[40]

Doubtless, the merely verbal commitment to maintain liberty must be reinforced by an arrangement of powers within the governmental structure such as has been outlined. Freedom of the press, too, has a role to play here. Ultimately, however, the defense of liberty must be vouchsafed to the public: the spirit and character of the people must be such that tyranny can be successfully resisted. It was for this reason that Constant supported the preservation, to whatever extent it was possible in the modern world, of the sentiment of regionalism. Total centralization of power and uniformity of legislation was one of the great—and unnecessary—evils of the contemporary world. Regionalism could well provide a counterweight to the drive for centralized control that was the essence of modern tyranny: "Les intérêts et les souvenirs qui naissent des habitudes locales contiennent un germe de résistance que l'autorité ne souffre qu'à regret, et qu'elle s'empresse de

[39] Ibid., pp. 114–191.

[40] *Œuvres*, p. 1232.

déraciner. Elle a meilleur marché des individus ; elle roule sur eux sans efforts son poids énorme, comme sur du sable."[41]

It is here—as part of the extra-constitutional bulwark of guarantees of freedom—that religion, too, takes its place in Constant's thought. It must be emphasized that this was not the only, nor even perhaps the primary, basis for Constant's sympathy with religious faith. Nevertheless, as will become apparent, Constant came increasingly to the conclusion as time went on that religious faith was a necessary condition for the continued existence of a free society.

In order to understand Constant's position on religion and liberty, an appreciation of his reasons for rejecting the ethics of utility is indispensable. As with Acton and other anti-utilitarian liberals of the nineteenth century, Constant draws a sharp contrast between utility and duty, between hedonism and the willingness to sacrifice for an ideal. Again and again, throughout his mature period, he castigates hedonism and the morality of rightly understood self-interest as ethically invalid and politically dangerous, as well as objectionable on a number of other grounds. It has been well said of him that "Cet individualiste à outrance dévient presqu'un socialiste, quand il parle des funestes conséquences que doivent produire l'"égoïsme et l'intérêt personnel érigés en maxime."[42]

In Benjamin Constant's continuing dialogue with the French Enlightenment, his distaste for its typical ethical perspective is one of the recurrent notes. He always associated self-interest as the basis of ethics with the eighteenth century, and, for him, many of that era's characteristic errors in politics, social theory, and, indeed, in its whole approach to life, are intimately connected with its mistaken ethical position. This is clear, for instance, from his diagnosis of M. de Maltigues, the cynical and malicious villain of Madame de Staël's *Corinne*:

> [Il] est le résultat d'un siècle où l'on a dit que la morale n'était qu'un calcul bien entendu, et qu'il fallait surtout jouir de la vie ; où l'on a créé contre tous les genres d'enthousiasmes le mot puissant de "niaiserie."[43]

[41] Ibid., p. 1015.

[42] Saltet, op. cit., pp. 36–37.

[43] Benjamin Constant, *Mélanges de littérature et de politique* (Paris : Pichon et Didier, 1829), pp. 185–196.

Although his manifold criticisms of this ethical view are scattered throughout his works, it is possible to arrange them so as to present a rather formidable attack on utilitarianism.

The most fundamental criticism Constant makes is that pleasure per se is not an ethically relevant value. This position is already suggested in his conception of the proper end of man: that end, as he reiterates, is the "moral perfectioning" of the individual. Constant, like Acton after him, maintains that the categories of hedonism have in the last analysis nothing to do with those of ethics. The enjoyment of pleasure is a morally neutral event; it may be said to pertain to the sphere of natural occurrences, comparable to the functioning of animals. In adopting the "morality" of hedonism:

> vous ferez de l'homme de plus habile, le plus droit, le plus sagace des animaux ; mais vous le placerez en vain au sommet de cette hiérarchie matérielle : il n'en restera pas moins au-dessous du dernier échelon de toute hiérarchie morale. Vous le jetterez dans une autre sphère que celle où vous croyez l'appeler.[44]

In this, Constant was decisively influenced, after his youthful adherence to a fashionable philosophical hedonism, by the ethics of Kant. His conversion to this approach in ethics seems to date from 1794, when, after a sojourn in Brunswick, he came to the conclusion that German philosophy was to be preferred to French and English, and he declared to Madame de Charrière that he had been persuaded of the notion of "le devoir absolu et indépendant, et par là même simple," in the sense of Kant.[45] Although he was later to have a fairly celebrated altercation in print with the latter over the question of whether the obligation to tell the truth is, in fact, unconditional, he never rejected the basic exclusion of pleasure from ethical philosophy, and his rejection of utilitarian-type ethical systems, even later, relies to some extent on certain Kantian ethics.

On the question of what effects would be incurred by the adoption of hedonism as a basis of morality, Constant's opinion varied to some degree. At times he gave the appearance of merely asserting that an ethic openly proclaiming the maximization of utility or pleasure as the sole *raison d'être*

---

[44] *De la religion*, vol. 1, p. xxxix. (Italics added.)

[45] B. Muntaneo, "Episodes Kantiens en Suisse et en France," *Revue de Littérature Comparée* 25 (1935), p. 444.

of moral rules would tend to produce certain practical difficulties. On at least one occasion he suggests that his quarrel is not so much with the principle that what is useful is what ought to be sought after, but with the too limited conception of what might prove to be useful to man. Thus, he notes in the *Journaux* that it is a short-sighted view that holds that the pursuit of theology in past centuries was a complete waste of human energies, for this discipline, "quoique partant de principes faux," developed certain valuable intellectual traits. From this he concludes: "Tout ce qui exerce l'esprit est bon, et il est même dangereux à quelques égards de trop rechercher si le but est utile. A force de ne vouloir que l'utilité, on élague mille choses dont on méconnaît l'utilité indirecte."[46]

The limits of Constant's readiness to compromise with utilitarianism is reached in his statement concerning the ideas of "droit" and "utilité": "Ce n'est qu'une différence de rédaction," he writes, "mais elle est plus importante qu'on ne pense."[47] Constant concedes that if the term "utility" is suitably defined, there is no doubt that a utilitarian ethic will generate the same moral rules as an ethic based on natural law and justice; it will always be found, on careful examination, that what is not just is also not useful. But, he adds:

> Il n'en est pas moins vrai que le mot d'*utilité*, suivant l'acception vulgaire, rappelle une notion différente de celle de la justice ou du droit. Or, lorsque l'usage et la raison commune attachent à un mot une signification déterminée, il est dangereux de changer cette

[46] *Œuvres*, p. 424. An analogous idea is presented in one of the later volumes of *De la religion*: "useless" rules enjoined by a religion have the merit of habituating man to "ne pas se proposer dans tout ce qu'il fait un but ignoble et rapproché. Il est *utile* que l'homme se prescrive quelquefois des devoirs inutile." *De la religion*, vol. 4, pp. 487–488. (Italics added.)

[47] On this point we may compare Dicey: "The privileges ... of the nobles under the *Ancient Régime* were in 1789 palpably opposed to the welfare of the French people. Bentham would have said that they were opposed to the principle of utility. A French reformer would have alleged that they were opposed to the law of nature. But this difference of language was at bottom little more than a different way of describing one and the same fact, viz., that the welfare of France required the establishing of equal civil rights among Frenchmen. Towards the close, indeed, of the eighteenth century, appeals to the doctrine of utility, and appeals to the law of nature were often in reality, though not in words, appeals to one and the same principle." A. V. Dicey, *Lectures on the Relation between Law and Public Opinion in England During the Nineteenth Century* (London: Macmillan, 1905), pp. 143–144.

> signification ; on explique vainement ensuite ce qu'on a voulu dire ; le mot reste, et l'explication s'oublie.[48]

Here Constant seems to be foregoing any principled objection to utilitarianism, and appears to base the superiority of the natural law position on the supposition that, if moral rules are couched in those terms, it is more likely that they will be followed. His fundamental position, however, is much more radical: it is that any system based on a pleasure and pain calculus is thoroughly subversive of morality.

This view stems from the 1790s, when, as has been pointed out, Constant accepted the basic tenets of the Kantian critique on this issue. At that time, he summed up his objections as follows:

> Si le bonheur général ou particulier est la pierre de touche du devoir, il est impossible de déterminer ce qu'est ce dernier. Non seulement le bonheur peut être variable en lui-même, mais il est nécessairement différent dans l'imagination de chaque individu. Le devoir est donc un être moulé au gré de chaque tête individuelle. Il y a plus : le devoir, devenant un calcul de bonheur, n'est plus un devoir. . . . Ainsi la morale fondée sur le bonheur n'a aucune base fixe. Le devoir ou le bien moral doit être absolument étranger aux circonstances et aux calculs. Ce doit être une idée isolée, indépendante et immuable ou ce n'est qu'un mot vide de sens et susceptible de tous les sens partiels que les passions, la courte vue ou l'exaltation peuvent lui donner.[49]

At the time he went on to express his doubts that such an exalted conception of morality was fitting for men as history and experience shows them to be. But, while this last notion fell away with the fading of his youthful cynicism, we see a number of his basic objections to hedonistic ethics (both, we should note, egoistic and social utilitarianism), which will remain with him and form a crucial element in his social thought. The arguments contained in this lengthy passage were elaborated by Constant at other times.

Thus he asserts that utilitarianism does not provide sufficiently unambiguous rules to serve as guides for moral action. For example, in dealing with cases in which I violate my neighbor's rights,

---

[48] *Mélanges*, pp. 143–144.

[49] Muntaneo, loc. cit., p. 444.

> si je ne juge de cette violation que par son utilité, *je puis me tromper dans mon calcul, trouver de l'utilité dans cette violation.* Le principe de l'utilité est par conséquence *bien plus* vague que celui du droit naturel.[50]

Here, it ought to be pointed out, Constant seems to have in mind the doctrine of *act* utilitarianism, for in classical utilitarianism of the Benthamite variety—a form of *rule* utilitarianism—one is not customarily in the position of having to pass judgment on the utility of violating someone else's rights. The system of (legal) rights has been established, presumably in accordance with the principle of the maximization of utility, and the individual is called upon simply to identify the case as one involving certain rights.

But, in reality, Constant's attack is on utilitarianism per se. A vital claim of his—although he does not use the terminology—is that there is a tendency for *rule* utilitarianism to degenerate into *act* utilitarianism:

> Sans doute, il est utile pour les transactions générales des hommes entre eux qu'il existe entre les membres des rapports immuables ; mais si l'on prétendait que ces rapports n'existent que parce qu'il est utile que cela soit ainsi, *on ne manquerait pas d'occasions où l'on prouverait qu'il serait infiniment plus utile de faire plier ces rapports*; on oublierait que leur utilité constante vient de leur immutabilité, et cessant d'être immuables, ils cesseraient d'être utiles.

From this he concludes, "Ce n'est que lorsque la règle est démontrée, qu'il est bon de faire ressortir l'utilité qu'elle peut avoir."[51] There is thus a tendency within utilitarianism to undermine its own foundation. This operates both on the level of private morality and of political morality ("il en est ainsi de la morale et du droit"). On the level of private morality, it may be pointed out that, human nature being what it is, it is likely that unless morality is established as deducible from an objective code, people are apt to decide moral questions in favor of their momentary desires: "l'évaluation d'un profit est arbitraire : c'est l'imagination qui en décide ; mais ni ses erreurs, ni ses caprices ne sauraient changer la notion du devoir."[52] Utilitarianism runs the constant danger of seeing its moral code

[50] *Mélanges*, p. 142. (Italics added.)
[51] Ibid., pp. 142–143. (Italics added.)
[52] Ibid., p. 144.

founder on the reef of human susceptibility to temptation. Moreover, it promotes this danger, for the term "utility" itself appeals to desire rather than to duty. The English utilitarians, Constant suggests, were not as perceptive as Helvétius in this regard; they overestimated the power of reason, even reason devoted to the calculation of one's own self-interest, to inhibit present passions from recklessly seeking their satisfaction. Of Helvétius, Constant writes:

> [Il] est beaucoup moins inconséquent que ses successeurs ne l'ont été. Admirateur des passions, il n'exhorte nulle part ses disciples à les vaincre.... Il donne l'intérêt pour mobile, mais il ne prétend pas le dénaturer par une épithète [i.e., " bien entendu "], et l'investir d'une sagesse, d'une prévoyance qu'il n'aura jamais.[53]

The same tendency for utilitarian ethics to degenerate into moral chaos operated on the political level. Here Constant doubtless had in mind above all the Terror, which he had condemned even in his republican and rationalist period. Judicial forms (one type of moral rule on the political level) had been systematically violated by virtue of the maxim *salus populi suprema lex esto*. To take social utility as the supreme standard, therefore, is to invite the breaking of rules which, while they do not openly declare it, do tend to maximize social welfare. Constant sometimes takes the position, then, that while rule utilitarianism is abstractly an acceptable ethic, in practice it must give away to act utilitarianism, which ultimately destroys all moral rules. An ethical code based on natural law will in application prove far more effective than one derived from utility, for "en parlant du droit, vous présentez une idée indépendante de tout calcul ; en parlant de l'utilité, vous semblez inviter à remettre la chose en question, en la soumettant à une vérification nouvelle."[54]

A somewhat more original objection to the hedonistic approach is contained in Constant's idea that—contrary to the typical view of writers such as Helvétius and the Philosophical Radicals, among others—the search for pleasure does *not* in fact constitute the only, or even the chief, stimulus to action in man. Here Constant appears to be rejecting the psychological claims on which utilitarianism is customarily based, although unfortunately he does not provide an altogether clear or systematic attack.

---

[53] *De la religion*, vol. 1, p. xxxi, n.

[54] *Mélanges*, p. 145.

The point in question is raised in the course of a passage in *De l'esprit de conquête* in which Constant sets forth the lethal consequences of arbitrary government for many lines of human activity. And it is not only in the arts and sciences that these consequences will be felt, he asserts. Commerce, too, will suffer:

> Le commerce n'est pas à lui seul un mobile d'activité suffisant ; l'on s'exagère l'influence de l'intérêt personnel ; l'intérêt personnel a besoin pour agir de l'existence de l'opinion : l'homme dont l'opinion languit étouffée, n'est pas longtemps excité, même par son intérêt ; une sorte de stupeur s'empare de lui . . . L'intérêt, séparé de l'opinion, est borné dans ses besoins, et facile à contenter dans ses jouissances : il travaille juste ce qu'il faut pour le présent, mais ne prépare rien pour l'avenir.[55]

To this we may add a passage which occurs in a talk delivered to the Athénée Royal of Paris, in 1819, in which Constant stated:

> D'ailleurs, Messieurs, est-il donc si vrai que le Bonheur de quelque genre qu'il puisse être soit le but unique de l'espèce humaine ? En ce cas, notre carrière serait bien étroite, et notre destination bien peu relevée. Il n'est pas un de nous qui, s'il voulait descendre, restreindre ses facultés morales, rabaisser ses désire, adjurer l'activité, la gloire, les émotions généreuses et profondes, ne pût s'abrutir et être heureux.

He adds, characteristically, that "ce n'est pas au Bonheur seul, c'est au perfectionnement que notre destin nous appelle."[56]

What Constant appears to be saying in these passages is that the reductive model of man set up by Helvétius and Bentham is fundamentally inadequate. It is not the case that, as Helvétius had asserted, "Corporeal sensibility is therefore [in the last analysis] the sole mover of men."[57] Or as Bentham had proclaimed: "Nature has placed mankind under the governance of two sovereign masters, pain and pleasure. It is for them alone to point out what we ought to do, as well as to determine what we shall do."[58]

---

[55] *Œuvres*, p. 1067.

[56] *Cours de politique constitutionnelle*, vol. 1, p. 559.

[57] Cited in Frederick Copleston, *A History of Philosophy* (London: Burns and Oates, 1960), vol. 6, p. 36.

[58] Jeremy Bentham, *The Principles of Morals and Legislation* (New York: Hafner, 1965), p. 1.

If this were in fact true, then we should expect a world peopled by *roués* and *bons vivants*, who indulge in the most easily obtainable and obvious pleasures; or rather (since even for such persons much of their pleasure is attributable in the last analysis to some sort of social "opinion"), we should expect a world of self-made brutes. Moreover, it would be the aim of rational men to make themselves into such beings. But, in spite of this, there are many, and they are acknowledged to be the best, who choose instead lines of action that either promise little or no pleasure, or pleasure which is uncertain and not clearly greater than the probable pain. This fact, Constant believes, simply cannot be explained by the psychological model erected by hedonists of whatever school.

Constant's view of the very limited effectiveness of pleasure seeking as a spur to (or an explanation of) action is reflected also in his description of a society organized and animated according to the principle of rightly understood self-interest. This would, he asserts, represent

> un état de choses où rien ne dérange le calcul ; où l'intérêt bien entendu, tranquille et sans effroi, sait toujours ce qu'il doit vouloir, et parvient toujours à se faire entendre. C'est le beau idéal d'une société gouvernée par cet intérêt bien entendu. Qu'a-t-elle de plus que les rassemblements industrieux des castors, ou les réunions bien ordonnées des abeilles ?[59]

Men are kept from this sort of fate, however, by the existence of a natural desire for and urge towards glory. As Constant puts it:

> C'était une belle conception de la nature d'avoir placé la récompense de l'homme hors de lui, d'avoir allumé dans son cœur cette flamme indéfinissable de la gloire, qui, se nourrissant de nobles espérances, source de toutes les actions grandes, préservatif contre tous les vices, lien des générations entre elles et de l'homme avec l'univers, repousse les désirs grossiers, et dédaigne les plaisirs sordides.[60]

We ought to note also that this passage clearly implies Constant's rejection of the psychological model of man which endows his psyche with a minimal naturally-given content; this insistence on the existence of "innate"

[59] *De la religion*, vol. 1, pp. xxxvi–xxxvii. As we shall see, this was the same kind of nightmare vision of the world of the future—conditioned solely by hedonistic motives—that so alarmed Tocqueville.

[60] *Œuvres*, pp. 1071–1072.

motives other than that of pleasure seeking will reappear in his concept of "le sentiment religieux."[61]

For Constant, however, the most serious problem presented by hedonistic ethics is not their incapacity to prevent crime or their tenuous psychological foundation, but rather lies in the debasement of human character they would inevitably effect, once having become generally accepted. Recent historical experience furnished both an illustration of what he had in mind and a certain amount of evidence for this thesis: he seems to have assumed that hedonism "reigned without rival" for about the whole period from the fall of Robespierre to the fall of Napoleon. Its effects were not difficult to discern: "cette indifférence, cette servilité, cette persistance dans le calcul, cette versatilité dans les prétextes, qu'était-ce autre chose que l'intérêt bien entendu."[62]

This state of public opinion was not an accidental one. Psychologically speaking, nothing more was to be expected. The followers of Helvétius are faced with a dilemma: if enlightened self-interest is not a powerful enough force to overcome the often furious passions which lead to crime, then it does not perform the first function of an ethical code. But if it is powerful enough for that, then it will certainly find it an easy matter to suppress the more subtle promptings of pity, generosity, tenderness and other altruistic emotions. In fact, if self-interest were accepted universally, we could expect the eventual drying up of these motives. "Il n'y a pas un noble sentiment du Cœur contre lequel la logique de l'intérêt bien entendu ne puisse s'armer."[63] Constant's indignation in this connection goes so far as to touch even the doctrines of the classical economists, which otherwise he treated as demonstrated scientific truth. He attacks both excessively rigorous poor laws, aimed at making the acceptance of poor relief as unattractive as possible, and the crusade against early marriages and large families on the part of the poor:

> On s'est interdit l'aumône qui vient de l'attendrissement et de la pitié ; on a ravi au pauvre sa liberté en échange de sa subsistance ;

[61] This is in accord with Constant's general rejection of the *tabula rasa* view; cf., *Mélanges*, pp. 213–214.

[62] *De la religion*, vol. 1, p. xxx.

[63] Cf., Constant remarks concerning the ruthlessness of the modern army of conquest, animated solely by self-interest: "Le calcul aurait tué dans leur âme toutes les émotions naturelles, excepté celles qui naissent de la sensualité." *Œuvres*, vol. 1, pp. xxiv–xxv.

> on s'est cru bienfaisant, quand sous des verroux on lui donnait du pain ... on a reproché à l'indigent ses penchants naturels, et à ses enfants leur existence ... on a transformé la vie en un parc, que ses propriétaires ont droit de clore du murs, et dont l'entrée n'est accordée que sous le bon plaisir de leur tolérance.[64]

The stanching of benevolent feelings towards others, however, does not simply retard the full ethical development of the individual. It has, in addition, quite serious consequences in social and political life, consequences of the sort that necessarily aroused the deepest concern in Constant. For the doctrine of self-interest, in his view, directly endangered the maintenance of a free society.

Again, we are obligated to mention the existence of a certain ambivalence in his thought on this question. On one occasion, at least, Constant emphasizes the *positive* value for freedom in the attachment of individuals to their own pleasure. This occurs in the case of the English, of whom he states:

> Le peuple le plus attaché à sa liberté, dans les temps modernes, est aussi le peuple le plus attaché à ses jouissances ; et il tient à sa liberté surtout, parce qu'il est assez éclairé pour y apercevoir la garantie de ses jouissances.[65]

This assertion implies that given a certain high degree of public enlightenment—sufficient to enable a very large number of individuals to comprehend the interconnectedness of a free political order and an abundant supply of enjoyments—the hedonistic approach would tend to provide a strong support for a free society. As will appear below, Tocqueville at one time expanded this argument into the position that *most* of the problems of a liberal order could be resolved through the enlightened self-interest of the citizens. But, as with Tocqueville, the main thrust of Constant's thought is towards undermining the force of this concession.

The argument that hedonism works against the preservation of a liberal order is ultimately founded on the claim that naked self-interest is subversive of mutual concern among the members of society in general. In Constant's words:

[64] *De la religion*, vol. 1, pp. xxiv–xxv.
[65] *Œuvres*, p. 1048.

> Il faut aux hommes, pour qu'ils s'associent réciproquement à leurs destinées, autre chose que l'intérêt. Il leur faut une opinion ; il leur faut de la morale. L'intérêt tend à les isoler, parce qu'il offre à chacun la chance d'être seul plus heureux ou plus habile.[66]

The ethic of self-interest, in fact, encourages each man to look upon himself as a pleasure machine, prudently husbanding his store of utility, and interested in others only to the extent that contact with them is likely to maximize his own pleasure. Such an attitude, if it were generally adopted, would result in insurmountable problems for the operation of the system of guarantees in the fact of governmental tyranny, for "ce n'est pas avec de tels éléments qu'un peuple l'obtient [i.e., liberty], la fonde ou la conserve."[67] The natural effect of the doctrine of self-interest

> est de faire que chaque individu soit son propre centre. Or, quand chacun est son propre centre, tous sont isolés. Quand tous sont isolés, il n'y a que de la poussière. Quand l'orage arrive, la poussière est de la fange.[68]

A consequence of complete egoism (or of "individualism," as Tocqueville was to call this tendency), Constant holds, is the emergence of an attitude of cold indifference to the fate of one's fellows; his conception of the future army of conquest, bred in an atmosphere of egoism (for such is the spirit of the times), is illuminating here. In the case of defeat, for instance:

> Chacun verrait, dans son camarade à l'agonie un dédommagement au pillage devenu impossible contre l'étranger.... L'infirme et le blessé paraîtraient à l'officier chargé de leur sort un poids importun dont il se débarrasserait à tout prix.[69]

And if the commanding general finds himself in a situation which cannot be salvaged, he will simply leave his men in the lurch; it is of no importance to him that they put their lives into his hands, trusting to his words. Instead, he will think: "Instruments inutiles, ne faut-il pas qu'ils soient brisés ?"[70] This rather overdrawn picture can perhaps best be understood not as a categorical prediction but as a depiction of the logical consequences of the doctrine of integral egoism.

---

[66] *Œuvres*, p. 998.
[67] *De la religion*, vol. 1, p. xxxvii.
[68] Ibid.
[69] *Œuvres*, p. 998.
[70] Ibid.

As has been indicated, Constant held that he had concrete evidence for the social effects of egoism in the recent history of France; the period following Thermidor, when hedonism was the order of the day in France, and especially in Paris, was one in which people had "laissé tomber les têtes et garanti les propriétés … empêché le pillage et facilité le meurtre légal."[71]

Given this perspective on hedonistic ethics, we can quite easily understand Constant's passion to demolish it, particularly when we note his view of the main tendencies of modern society, the "ideas" which lay at the base of contemporary society. A certain danger point, he held, had been reached in the progress of Western civilization, one which is inevitably attained in every progressive culture. In a conversation in 1814 with James Mackintosh, Constant advanced the thesis that

> every particular form of civilization, by multiplying the number of enjoyments which may be attained without reason or virtue, tends to its own destruction; that the mental qualities are destroyed, and the mechanical products only remain; that a foreign force is necessary to revive such a civilization—like the invasion of the barbarians, which supplied mental energy, while all the outward results of ancient civilization were preserved to be the instruments of that energy.[72]

Although Constant does not, in his published works, present the argument in this particular form, the basic sentiment is one that recurs often. The trend is, he states, the natural result of civilization to render "les jouissances plus faciles, plus variées et l'habitude que l'homme contracte de ces jouissances lui en fait un besoin qui le détourne de toutes les pensées élevées et nobles."[73] This is actually the undesirable reverse side of one which underlies the main argument of *De l'esprit de conquête.* There he argued that modern social and economic conditions have multiplied the sources of pleasure many fold, leading to a disinclination to engage in war (which was no longer materially profitable, and could only endanger and restrict the variety of possible pleasures):

[71] Quoted in Fabre-Luce, op. cit., p. 203

[72] James Macintosh, *Memoirs* (Boston: Little, Brown, 1853), vol. 2, p. 327. This is a rather extreme form of the idea under discussion. That an advanced civilization requires something like the barbarian invasions to revivify it was probably a notion that Constant toyed with at the time, and was willing to defend for the sake of argument; it does not constitute part of his general system of thought. On the contrary, see his essay, "De la perfectabilité de l'espèce humaine," in *Mélanges*, pp. 387–415.

[73] *De la religion*, vol. 1, p. xli, n.

> comme ces jouissances et la facilité que l'homme trouve à les obtenir attachement chacun à la position qui les lui assure, il est évident que chacun éprouve plus de répugnance à risquer cette position, même quand le devoir l'y invite.[74]

But this tendency towards civic passivity and pacifism brings with it at least two unfortunate consequences. The first is that it tends to lead to an overestimation of the value of order and stability in society, for the individual will hesitate to risk the desirable position he has attained:

> Or, le bon ordre, chose utile, chose indispensable aux progrès et à la prospérité des sociétés, est plutôt un moyen qu'un but. Si, pour le maintenir, on sacrifie toutes les émotions généreuses, on réduit les hommes à un état peu différent de celui de certains animaux industrieux, dont les ruches bien ordonnés et les cases artistement construites ne sauraient pourtant être le beau idéal de l'espèce humaine.[75]

Such an overvaluation of stability would thus produce a state of stagnation both of society and of the individual; its tendency is towards the brutalization of man, not so much in the sense that he will become overly aggressive or murderous, but in the opposite sense, that of, say, Aldous Huxley's *Brave New World.*

Secondly, undue emphasis on order necessarily implies acquiescence in the coming to power of the strongest faction, the one best able to preserve order. For power is always able to promise that it will preserve social order, and this is usually enough for the principle of self-interest to rush to enlist itself on its side.[76] Moreover, the same love of ease and comfort that now makes it unlikely that men will go to war implies a decline in civic spirit and civic courage which is very dangerous from the viewpoint of liberty:

> Le plus imminent de ces dangers [those resulting from the tendency of civilization] est une espèce de résignation fondée sur le calcul, et qui, balançant les inconvénients des résistances avec les inconvénients des transactions, nuit également et au maintien de la liberté contre le despotisme intérieur, et à la défense de l'indépendance contre les invasions étrangers.[77]

---

[74] *Mélanges*, p. 134.
[75] Ibid., p. 135.
[76] *De la religion*, vol. 1, pp. xxxi–xxxii.
[77] *Mélanges*, p. 135.

Again, the period of Napoleonic tyranny provides Constant with evidence for his thesis. He points out that the two countries where Napoleon's triumphal march was reversed, Spain and Russia, were countries quite backward materially. In addition, he finds it significant that in Spain it was the lower class (for whom material benefits were less accessible) who fought the invading French armies tooth and nail, while the upper classes were rather willing to yield.[78]

For Constant, the modern frame of mind represented a grave peril indeed. From the perspective of his "state hatred" (or, at least, deep distrust of the state), it must be assumed that the holders of political power by and large will always be engaged in at least a cold war against the rights of man. Thus, resistance to governmental encroachments will often be required, and sometimes it will even be necessary for some, at least, to risk their lives in the struggle. But it will most often not be the case that the individual who rises to resist authority will thereby win for himself a position comfortable enough to compensate him for his pains. And as for the cases when one's very life must be risked, it is hardly consistent with egoistic hedonism for the individual to seriously risk his life for *anything* whatsoever, particularly for an abstract cause. In consequence, on the basis of enlightened self-interest alone, the chances for the preservation of a free society are dim indeed.

Thus Constant raises the problem of modern "materialism," of the effects of affluence, and especially of the proliferation of creature comforts, on the personality and character of man and on the prospects for a free society. Somehow an antidote to this tendency of civilization must be found:

> Il est donc important de contre-balancer cet effet de la civilisation, en recueillant et en entretenant, le plus qu'il est possible, les sentiments nobles et désintéressés ... tâchons de conserver au sein de la civilisation les idées nobles, les émotions généreuses que les jouissances tendent à étouffer.[79]

In view, then, of the multitudinous difficulties inherent in hedonistic ethics, it was imperative that some sort of alternative be found. In Constant's mind, it was clear what the alternative had to be. As he states in *De la religion*:

[78] Ibid., p. 139.
[79] Ibid., p. 135.

> Tous les systèmes [morales] se réduisent à deux. L'un nous assigne l'intérêt pour guide, et le bien-être pour but. L'autre nous propose pour but le perfectionnement, et pour guide le sentiment intime, l'abnégation de nous-mêmes et la faculté de sacrifice.[80]

The end, of course, as stated above, is the somewhat vague notion of the perfectioning of the individual. It must be pointed out, however, that the means to the discovery of which actions conduce to this ethical goal and which do not is stated to be not the intellect, as Constant elsewhere give cause to suppose, but some interior feeling. The contradiction this involves for Constant's thought requires some explanation.

At times, particularly in his earlier work, Constant tended to the conception of ethics of writers such as Locke and Montesquieu (among others): of the Locke who maintained that "morality is capable of demonstration, as well as mathematics,"[81] and of the Montesquieu who, also making use of the mathematical model, asserted, "Dire qu'il n'y a rien de juste ni d'injuste que ce qu'ordonnent ou défendent les lois positives, c'est dire qu'avant qu'on eût tracé de cercle, tous les rayons n'étaient pas égaux."[82] Occasionally, Constant also conceives of morality in such rationalistic terms, as a collection of rules or "laws" discoverable by reason. This seems clearly to be implied in the passages already quoted, which speak of "demonstrating" the ethical rule, and which attack making happiness the basis of ethics because in that case duty would vary with the individual imagination. His final and mature view, however, or at least that which is most unambiguously set forth in *De la religion*, appears to be an intuitionist one, rather than a rationalist one:

> Non, la nature n'a point placé notre guide dans notre intérêt bien entendu, mais dans notre sentiment intime. Ce sentiment nous avertit de ce qui est mal ou de ce qui est bien. L'intérêt bien entendu ne nous fait connaître que ce qui est avantageux ou ce qui est nuisible.[83]

Considering Constant's lack of philosophical sophistication, it is not surprising that at times the two conceptions are even intermingled. In any

[80] *De la religion*, vol. 1, pp. xxxviii–xxxix.

[81] Cited in Alasdair MacIntyre, *A Short History of Ethics* (New York: Macmillan, 1966), p. 160.

[82] Montesquieu, op. cit., bk. 1, chap. 1.

[83] *De la religion*, vol. 1, pp. xxvi–xxvii.

case, it is not necessary for us to attempt to square these two notions. The rationalist one may perhaps best be regarded as an unexamined residue in his thinking, left over from an earlier period. The more important one, in respect to the question of the connection of religion to other social forces, is the intuitionist and romantic perspective on ethics.

Benjamin Constant occupied himself for about forty years with his work on religion,[84] and if it is too much to say, as does a recent commentator, that for Constant "die Religion den eigentlichen Schlüssel zum Verständnis der Menscheitsentwicklung bilde,"[85] it is nevertheless obvious that he considered religion of very great importance.

Constant's own religious views underwent something of the same change during his life as his ideas on related subjects: that is, they manifest an evolution away from eighteenth-century rationalism towards a more romantic position. While in his early work, *Des réactions politiques* (1796), he could, in good Girondin style, treat of religion under the name of "fanaticism,"[86] in a few years he began demonstrating distaste for standard anti-religious thinking. As early as 1805 he states in his diary that "il y a dans l'irréligion quelque chose de grossier et d'usé qui me répugne."[87] Significantly, by that date he was able to add: "D'ailleurs, j'ai mon coin de religion. Mais il est tout en sentiment, en émotions vagues : il ne peut se réduire en système."[88] Constant was aware of the directions his thinking was taking. At one time he wrote to Claude Hochet: "Mon ouvrage est une singulière preuve de ce que dit Bacon, qu'un peu de science mène à l'athéisme, et plus de science à la religion."[89] But although his religious feelings were urgent enough at times to lead him to toy with mysticism, and despite his profession of faith as a Protestant,[90] the degree to which he

[84]Saltet, op. cit., p. 11.
[85]Gall, op. cit., p. 118.
[86]Asse, loc. cit., pp. 354–355.
[87]*Œuvres*, p. 469.
[88]Ibid.
[89]Cited in Gall, op. cit., p. 118.
[90]At one point he speaks of "le protestantisme que nous professions." *De la religion*, vol. 1, p. 16, n.

ever achieved real religious faith in any traditional sense is questionable.[91] At best, it was the sort of liberal Protestantism which was coming to the fore in Germany that claimed his allegiance, and that he described in the following terms:

> Chaque jour la religion protestante déviant en Allemagne plus une chose de sentiment qu'une institution : point de forme, point de symbole, rien d'obligatoire, presque point de cérémonie, rien que des idées douces et une morale sensible.[92]

In a sense, Constant's strong assertion of the indispensability of religion gains in interest in view of his own lack of traditional religious commitment.

One of the basic conclusions Constant had been led to in his study of religion was the impossibility of an atheistic society existing for any length of time. This motion is perhaps best understood as a reaction against the atheist worldview of a d'Holbach or a La Mettrie, the full implications of which had been glimpsed by Constant and which had filled him with horror. A race that accepted them would, he believed, confront a world drained of all traces of humanity: "L'univers est sans vie : des générations passagères, fortuites, isolées, y paraissent, souffrent, meurent : nul lien n'existe entre ces générations, dont le partage est ici la douleur, plus loin le néant."[93] Even egregious error in religious beliefs, even superstition (the *bête-noir* of the *philosophes*) was preferable to atheism.[94] Moreover, it appeared to be a fact of human nature that the atheistic conception of the universe was so horrible as to be unacceptable in the long run for the great mass of mankind. Both historical experience and "psychology" (in the form of Constant's concept of an innate religious sentiment) provide evidence on this point:

[91] Saltet, op. cit., p. 68; Gall, op. cit., pp. 119–120. Faguet goes too far in calling Constant "un homme sans aucun sentiment religieux, qui a écrit toute sa vie un livre sur la religion." Op. cit., p. 187.

[92] *Œuvres*, p. 264.

[93] Quoted in Gall, op. cit., p. 119.

[94] *De la religion*, vol. 1, p. xvi; vol. 2, p. 277.

> Historiquement, nous n'en voyons d'exemple nulle part [of the possibility of doing away with religion altogether]. Psychologiquement, l'existence du sentiment religieux nous semble y mettre obstacle. Les Romains se croyaient dans cette situation vers le premier siècle de notre ère. Trois cents ans plus tard, les convictions religieuses avaient pénétré de nouveau dans tous les esprits, la foi reconquis toutes les âmes.[95]

Indeed, an indication of the indestructibility of religious feelings is given by the materialists themselves, by "cet enthousiasme pour la nature, pour le grant tout," a sort of frantic adulation of the cosmos and its iron laws, which may be noted in certain of their writings. This, Constant declares, is nothing but "le sentiment religieux se reproduisant sous un autre nom au sein de l'athéisme lui-même."[96] Thus, in view of the inevitability of religion, the question becomes rather in what form it will establish itself.[97]

Turning to a consideration of the fundamental nature of religion, Constant begins by positioning a religious element in man which is innate and whose origin is subject to no further explanation. All beings exhibit certain distinctive modes of existence which constitute the nature of their species, modes which it would be fruitless to attempt to trace back to anterior causes, but which themselves are the starting point for any explanation of more specific phenomena associated with the species. In the case of man, among such fundamental conditions of his nature is the religious sentiment.[98] Constant holds that it is an error to try to trace the development of religious feeling to other causes, just as it is folly to seek for the origin of society or of language: all these are constituent elements of human nature, inherent in man.[99] It follows from this that those writers who have sought the first cause of religion in fear, ignorance, deceit, the urge to domination, etc., were mistaken. There is no more reason to have recourse to such explanations in this case than in the case of any other inherent human quality.[100]

The precise nature of "le sentiment religieux" remains somewhat vague, perhaps necessarily so. Constant defines it at one point as "le besoin que

[95] Ibid., vol. 5, pp. 167–168.
[96] Ibid., vol. 1, p. 49.
[97] Ibid, vol. 5, p. 173.
[98] Ibid., vol. 1, pp. 2–3.
[99] Ibid., vol. 1, p. 23.
[100] Ibid., vol. 1, p. 6.

l'homme éprouve de se mettre en communication avec la nature qui l'entoure, et les forces inconnues qui lui semblent animer cette nature."[101] Perhaps the best indication of what he had in mind is given by a passage from Lord Byron's poem, "Island," which Constant quotes in this connection because it furnishes "une définition tellement d'accord avec la nôtre." The poem begins with the lines:

> How often we forget all time, when lone,
> Admiring nature's universal throne,
> Her woods, her wilds, her waters, the intense
> Reply of hers to our intelligence!

And the last line quoted by Constant read: "Strip off this fond and false identity! / Who thinks of self, when gazing on the sky?"[102] It is highly significant that for Constant self-abnegation was of the essence of religious belief: "Ce que le Sauvage fait pour lui-même n'est que de l'égoïsme : ce qu'il fait pour les morts qu'il a aimés est de la religion."[103] This is one indication of the interconnection in his mind of religion and non-utilitarian ethics.

But if the religious sentiment is an expression of unchangeable human nature, this is not at all the case with the *forms* which it assumes. Here, Constant lays down a fruitful distinction, which will, as we shall see, assist him at critical points later on: while the religious sentiment is the need which man feels for communication with the transcendental realm, "la forme naît du besoin qu'il éprouve également de rendre réguliers et permanents les moyens de communication qu'il croit avoir découverts."[104] The religious sentiment thus pertains to the unchangeable essence of man, while the religious forms pertain to history.

We have already spoken of Constant's conception of the manner in which the interaction of newly emerging ideas and needs, on the one hand, and established institutions, on the other, produces first stresses and eventually modification in social institutions, serving to bring them into line with the contemporary *Zeitgeist*. This conception is most clearly

[101] Ibid., vol. 1, pp. 219–220.
[102] Ibid., vol. 1, p. 142, n.
[103] Ibid., vol. 1, p. 93.
[104] Ibid., vol. 1, p. 40.

articulated in his theory of the evolution of religious forms. As Constant expresses it, we find

> à chaque époque l'établissement d'une forme positive [of religion], proportionnée à l'état de cette époque. Mais toute forme positive, quelque satisfaisante qu'elle soit pour le présent, contient un germe d'opposition aux progrès de l'avenir.... Le sentiment religieux se sépare alors de cette forme pour ainsi dire pétrifiée. Il en réclame une autre qui ne le blesse pas, et il s'agite jusqu'à ce qu'il l'ait trouvée.[105]

The modifications in the social substructure which account for the changes in the religious superstructure comprise changes in thought, in moral awareness and, generally, in the state of development which society has so far reached. The dependence of religious forms on more fundamental social factors is an important part of Constant's theory:

> Nous avons établi, comme la vérité principale à démontrer dans notre ouvrage, que chaque révolution qui s'opère dans la situation de l'espèce humaine en produit une dans les idées religieuses.[106]

Constant finds evidence for his theory, and an interesting illustration of it, in the differences in the character of the gods as depicted in the *Iliad* and in the *Odyssey*. He accepts the position which had been advanced by the German scholar F. A. Wolf, according to which the two poems were composed by different authors. In Constant's view, a study of the social conditions which form the background of the two poems shows that they pertain to two different epochs. The *Odyssey* takes place in a social setting characterized by less war, the beginnings of legislation, the first attempts at commerce; in it, human relations manifest the partial replacement of force by reason and commerce, the germs of the conception of the rights of the citizen, and to some degree the pursuit of science.[107] This evolution in society led inevitably to a difference in the nature of the deities, a difference which may be noted in the two poems. In the earlier work, for instance, the gods are moved only by insults to their priests, by the neglect of the proper

---

[105] Ibid., vol. 1, pp. 41–42.

[106] Ibid., vol. 4, pp. 345–346. Cf., his statement: "Aussitôt qu'une révolution s'opère dans l'état de la race humaine, la religion subit un changement analogue." Ibid., vol. 2, p. 2.

[107] Ibid., vol. 3, pp. 416–418.

sacrifices to them, and by similar considerations, while in the *Odyssey*, the infraction of moral rules governing the relations of men among themselves is sometimes enough to bring down their wrath. As Constant puts it: "On dirait . . . que durant cet intervalle, leur [the gods'] éducation morale a fait des progrès."[108]

The changes in the other sectors of society lead, sooner or later, to changes in the forms of religious life. In Constant's statement, man, after establishing a religious form, "cette première nécessité de sa nature,"

> développe et perfectionne ses autres facultés. Mais ses succès mêmes rendent la forme qu'il avait donnée à ses idées religieuses disproportionnée avec ses facultés développées et perfectionnées. Dès ce moment, la destruction de cette forme est inévitable.[109]

This transformation of one religious form into another may be affected in one of two ways: "soit par les corporations de prêtres chez les nations soumises au sacerdoce, soit par les progrès de l'esprit humain chez les peuples indépendants de la puissance sacerdotale."[110] Constant thus introduces a distinction which is of the greatest importance for his whole theory of the development of religion, and which has been termed "l'idée-mère et ... la fin dernière" of his whole work.[111] As Constant himself asserts: "la distinction entre les religions soumises au sacerdoce et celles qui en sont indépendantes est la première condition requise pour concevoir des idées justes sur cette matière."[112]

This distinction is one which had been fermenting in Constant's mind for some time, and which can be traced back at least as far as the period in which his overall attitude towards religion began to become more sympathetic. Already in 1805 he noted in *Journaux* the importance of "la différence de la marche soumises aux prêtres et de celle des religions livrées à elles-mêmes."[113] Indeed, it may well be the case that it was the perception of this distinction that permitted Constant, the enemy of intolerance and persecution, to regard at least one category of religion with favor.

---

[108]Ibid., vol. 3, pp. 409–413.
[109]Ibid., vol. 1, p. 144.
[110]Ibid., vol. 1, p. 211.
[111]Saltet, op. cit., p. 61.
[112]*De la religion*, vol. 1, p. 210.
[113]*Œuvres*, p. 509.

We need not follow Constant in his development of the theme of the capture and exploitation of religious feelings by the priestly castes for its own purposes. Theirs was a power based principally on a monopoly of knowledge of the sciences[114] and associated, historically, with the worship of the stars and the elements.[115] Having analyzed out of the history of religion this one element, Constant proceeds to try to demonstrate that it was the priestly corporation that was responsible for most of the crimes, oppressive institutions, etc., which freethinkers had been accustomed to ascribe to religion per se. The notion of original sin,[116] the preservation of the caste system (which the passage of time would have dissolved),[117] the concept of diabolical powers operating within the human personality,[118] and the promotion of secular despotism,[119] are a few of the evils traceable to priestly power. The toll which this group of privileged individuals has taken through the ages is incalculable: "On peut difficilement aujourd'hui concevoir dans toute son étendue, le mal qu'a fait à l'homme le sacerdoce de l'antiquité."[120] The price of mankind's abdication of intelligence to these holy despots has been for centuries slavery, falsehood and fear.[121]

Constant pursues his prosecution of hedonistic ethics into the analysis of the historical development of religion. The influence of the priest throughout this development has been closely bound up with selfishness, with that of the worshippers as well as of the priests themselves.

There are two sorts of motives connected with religion on the part of the worshipper, Constant maintains. One, the religious sentiment properly so-called, we have already discussed: its essence is forgetfulness of self and concentration of the ego on others and on the cosmos. The other sort of motive, however, is "égoiste, ardent, mercenaire," desiring to take advantage of religion for personal advancement. It is this drive which

[114] *De la religion*, vol. 2, p. 112.

[115] Ibid., vol. 2, pp. 285–286.

[116] Ibid., vol. 4, p. 166.

[117] Ibid., vol. 2, p. 66.

[118] Ibid., vol. 4, pp. 159–161. Interestingly, Constant complains that this idea had led to a stopping up of spontaneous and natural emotions: "L'homme ne sait jamais si les mouvements de son Cœur, les élans de son âme, l'activité de son esprit ne sont pas les suggestions d'un pouvoir malin."

[119] Ibid., vol. 5, p. 194.

[120] Ibid., vol. 2, p. 465.

[121] Ibid., vol. 4, p. 42.

creates a need for priests, as the specialist in the arcane lore by which the gods are brought to serve human wants.[122] In their turn, the priests surrender to the desire for personal power. Any authentic religious feeling is destroyed within the priestly class, and at the core of the doctrine which the priests share only among themselves we find a religious void.[123]

From the point of view of the evolution of religion towards higher and more perfect forms, the priest plays the same role in Constant's conception as does the meddling political authority in the economic realm: by interfering with the free play of social forces, he prevents the equilibrium which nature would have brought about, and produces a host of evils as by-products:

> Au lieu de se développer et de s'épurer, le sentiment religieux, s'agitant sous des entraves contre nature, serait devenu désordonné, faute de progression ; délirant, faute de liberté.... Le polythéisme sacerdotal ... conserve à ses idoles toutes leurs difformités et tous leurs vices.[124]

In view of all this, Constant finds it difficult to overestimate the benefits for mankind from the circumstances that the Greeks did not permit the priestly caste to come to power.[125] The condition of laissez-faire obtaining in their religious life enabled them to benefit from the natural progress of science and morality to purify their religion; the latter was one "marchant d'un pas égal avec la morale, et s'épurant à mesure que l'intelligence de l'homme s'éclaire."[126]

The ultimate grounds for Constant's profound hostility to the priest —a distinguishing mark of his work among contemporary attempts to cast religious belief in a new light—are to be found in his basically anti-authoritarian orientation, which led him to distrust and resent hierarchy and organization per se, in the residue of the eighteenth-century philosophy and particularly in his fear of the consequences of the Catholic revival of the early nineteenth century.[127] In connection with this last point, at one time he thought he could even discern a sort of conspiracy at work:

---

[122]Ibid., vol. 1, pp. 343–344.
[123]Ibid., vol. 3, p. 21.
[124]Ibid., vol. 2, pp. 461–462
[125]Ibid., vol. 2, pp. 467–468.
[126]Ibid., vol. 3, p. 302.
[127]Saltet, op. cit., pp. 61–62.

> Il y a un plan bien suivi pour rétablir dans les sciences, dans les lettres, dans les comédies, dans les romans, la disposition d'esprit étroite et soumise qui favorise le catholicisme.... C'est un pari de certains hommes contre l'esprit humain. Je doute qu'ils le gagnent.[128]

This suspension of the political role of the Christian priest is reflected in Constant's work. Although he was at pains to distinguish the Christian clergy from the priestly castes of pagan religions, he noted also that "le judaïsme et le christianisme [had been] souvent défigurés par l'esprit sacerdotal,"[129] and attributed the fact that the priests of modern religions pose less of a danger to civilization due to strict limits set to their power.[130]

Thus, Constant's work on religion, with its conception of the role of the religious sentiment and of the priest, manifests the same tendency as much of his other writings: a path is conceptually hewn between the dangers of rationalism, radicalism, and the ideas of the *philosophes*, on the one hand, and the thought of the reactionary conservatives on the other. His conception of the proper policy on religion is much the same as his attitude towards other social institutions: "Laissons-la à Dieu et à elle-même. Toujours proportionnée, elle marchera avec les idées, s'éclairera avec la raison, s'épurera avec la morale, et à chaque époque, elle sanctionnera ce qu'il y aura de meilleur."[131]

In regard to the question of the connection between religion and morality, Constant maintained that they were logically and historically distinct: "il est très-possible pour le raisonnement de concevoir la religion séparée de la morale. Les relations des hommes avec les dieux constituent la religion. Les relations des hommes avec les hommes constituent la morale. Ces deux choses n'ont aucun rapport nécessaire entre elles."[132] Historically, a fusion between religion and morality occurred at a certain stage of social evolution. Here, Constant maintains, the role of the priest was again crucial, and societies divide in the manner in which and the stage at which

[128] *Œuvres.*, pp. 264–265.
[129] *De la religion*, vol. 4, p. 494.
[130] Ibid., vol. 1, pp. xi–xii.
[131] Ibid., vol. 5, pp. 206–207.
[132] Ibid., vol. 1, p. 273.

the fusion occurs, according as they are dominated by the priestly caste or are free in their religious development.

In religions under priestly influence, moral ideas very quickly become associated with religion; Constant attributes this to the priests' unquenchable thirst for power.[133] This has two very serious consequences for morality. In the first place, the moral code comes to be regarded as *promulgated* by the gods, not simply *sanctioned* by them. An element of arbitrariness is thus introduced into the very foundations of ethics: acts are no longer evil by their nature, but by the inscrutable will of a god.[134] Significantly, Constant attacks the Mosaic religion—which elsewhere he finds praiseworthy on a number of counts—precisely because of this:

> ces mots qui précédent et qui suivent presque toutes les lois : "Je suis l'Éternel, votre dieu, gardez mes commandements," ne peuvent se traduire que par cette paraphrase despotique : "Ces commandements peuvent vous paraître futiles ou contraire à vos idées du bien et du mal ; mais qu'il vous suffise que j'en sois l'auteur, moi, votre maître.[135]

The second major mischief which the priestly influence on morality accomplishes is to create a great body of bogus moral rules, whose purpose is either to solidify the priests' power or to further some other goal with no connection with any authentic ethical end, or, indeed, in direct contradiction to it. Here the priests debase the very idea and name of morality, and although the history of priests is a nasty one, this is perhaps the worst of their acts.[136] Moreover, the approach to morality which makes it a simple function of the will of the gods has the added danger of involving moral rules too intimately in the fate of organized religion. Thus, in the middle of the eighteenth century in France, Constant asserts: "Comme on avait donné pour base à la morale une religion positive, la chute de cette religion favorisait la licence." [137]

Constant does not deny, of course, that morality becomes associated naturally with religion in the course of social evolution, or that it is right and proper that this occur. What he insists on, however, is the superiority

[133] Ibid., vol. 4, pp. 101–102.
[134] Ibid., vol. 4, pp. 481–482.
[135] Ibid., vol. 4, p. 485, n.
[136] Ibid., vol. 4, pp. 102–103, 499–500.
[137] Ibid., vol. 5, p. 169.

of the manner in which religion and morality become linked in those religions not under the direction of priests. Here, morality has acquired an independent recognition, has become intertwined with all sorts of other attitudes and institutions, and thus is not susceptible of being made the instrument of priestly power. On the contrary, what we witness at the earliest stage of the connection of the two in this type of society is a purification of *religion.* As Constant puts it (his favorite example of this sort of evolution is the Greeks): "Les héros d'Homère sont encore supérieurs à leurs dieux." With the introduction of moral ideas into the religious concepts of the Greeks, the gods undergo a "moral education," and soon are imagined to be morally superior to men.[138] The beneficent influence of morality on religion is summed up by Constant: "Les dieux, comme les humains, se soumettent aux lois éternelles, et la conscience inviolable et respectée prononcé sur les volontés des uns, comme sur la conduite des autres."[139]

Parallel to the progress in religious ideas produced by morality, there is the influence which is exercised on morality by religion. Here Constant is at pains to emphasize, as part of his ongoing campaign against utilitarianism, that the utility of religion ought never to occupy first place in our considerations,[140] and that religion is not a penal code.[141] Nevertheless, he also states that although in the ideal case the gods are not conceived of as decreeing the moral code, they act as its guarantors.[142] Particularly in the case of oath taking, Constant finds the religious sanction indispensable. He depicts the terrible consequences of the disappearance of respect for oaths: "Alors tous les liens sont brisés ; le droit n'existe plus ; le devoir disparaît avec le droit ; la force est déchaînée ; le parjure fait de la société un état permanent de guerre et de fraude."[143] From the very beginning of society, it is religion which preserves men from these evils, by acting as a guarantor of oaths.[144]

Since Constant asserts both that religion acts as a guarantee of moral rules and that it ought not to be looked on as a supplement to the penal

---

[138] Ibid., vol. 3, pp. 403–404.
[139] Ibid., vol. 5, p. 180.
[140] For example, ibid., vol. 2, p. 274.
[141] Ibid., vol. 4, p. 503.
[142] Ibid., vol. 4, pp. 356–358, 474–475.
[143] Ibid., vol. 1, pp. 275–276.
[144] Ibid., vol. 1, pp. 276–278.

codes, it is difficult to know whether he believed that morality could be effectively enforced in the absence of religion. On the whole, his judgment seems to incline towards seeing a minimal sort of morality as possible even in the absence of religious sanctions. As he states: "Pour prévenir les attentats grossiers en les punissant, les lois et les châtiments suffisent." He sees the role of religious feelings in this sphere as pertaining more to the elevation of character by encouraging the higher virtues: "C'est pour changer l'intérieure de l'homme, au lieu d'arrêter seulement son bras, que le sentiment religieux est indispensable."[145] Constant's expression of his idea is at times vague and confusing; thus, he states, "la religion laisse aux lois leur juridiction sur les effets [of human action]: elle se borne à améliorer la cause."[146] Nevertheless, it seems tolerably certain that what he had in mind was something close to the attitude represented by John Stuart Mill about a generation later, in his essay, "On the Utility of Religion." The argument for religion based on its value "as a supplement to human laws, a more cunning sort of police, an auxiliary to the thief-catcher and the hangmen," was one he set out to demolish. Mill found much more plausible, however, the notion that "supernatural beliefs are ... necessary to the perfection of the individual character," although he went on to argue that traditional religions might be rendered superfluous by the introduction of a "religion of humanity."[147] Constant's view, then, may be summarized by saying that the most important consequence of an independent and advanced religion in regard to human conduct is not that it prevents crime, but it so acts on the mind of the believer that he becomes not only a person incapable of crime, but one inspired by noble and generous sentiments, and thus approaches the moral perfectioning that is the highest ethical goal.

The final element of the association of religion and morality which appears in Constant's thought is a *psychological* one. "La morale est un sentiment," he asserts, "Elle s'associe au sentiment religieux, parce que tous les sentiments se tiennent."[148] At another time he writes: "Il n'y a pas dans le cœur un bon sentiment qui ne perde à être séparé de la religion ; et s'il fallait choisir d'un peuple athée ou d'un peuple superstitieux, il n'y aurait

[145] Ibid., vol. 4, pp. 501–502.

[146] Ibid., vol. 4, p. 505.

[147] John Stuart Mill, *Nature and the Utility of Religion* (Indianapolis, Ind.: Bobbs-Merrill, 1958), pp. 62, 65–66.

[148] *De la religion*, vol. 1, p. 282.

pas à hésiter pour ce dernier."[149] This seems to imply that any attitude, such as that of the eighteenth-century materialists, which attacks the religious feeling, will tend also to weaken the ethical sentiment and is to be rejected on this ground as well.

Constant's strongest and most systematic statements on the necessity of religion to a free society are contained in the preface and the first chapters of his *De la religion considérée dans sa source, ses formes et ses développements*, published in 1824. Here he maintains, quite explicitly, that religion is a necessary, but not a sufficient, condition for the creation and preservation of a free society:

> Des peuples religieux ont pu être esclaves ; aucun peuple irréligieux n'est demeuré libre. La liberté ne peut s'établir, ne peut se conserver, que par le désintéressement, et toute morale étrangère au sentiment religieux ne saurait se fonder que sur le calcul. Pour défendre la liberté, on doit savoir immoler la vie, et qu'y a-t-il de plus que la vie pour qui ne voit au-delà que le néant ?[150]

We should note that this passage opens with what appears to be a historical generalization, but is not really that (as will be observed, Constant is often rather cavalier in citing "history" to support his conclusions on this subject). By his own statement, the sort of liberty he is concerned to preserve is an altogether modern thing, to be sharply distinguished from that of the classical republics.[151] There is therefore no obvious reason for supposing that the conditions for preserving what the moderns call "liberty" will be the same as those needed to maintain what went by that name among the ancients. Thus, it is not clear why, for instance, the history of the decline of settled faith among the Romans and their surrender to hedonism should enter into the question.[152] Moreover, as far as the modern nations are concerned, with one possible exception, Constant does not really have at his disposal the historical experience of any people which, having become irreligious, then lost its liberty. (The possible exception is

[149] Cited in Gall, op. cit., pp. 118–119.

[150] *De la religion*, vol. 1, p. 89.

[151] This point will be discussed in the following section.

[152] Ibid., vol. 1, pp. xl–xliv.

that of France from 1792 to the fall of Napoleon.) Thus, it is not so much on historical evidence as on insight into human psychology that Constant must rest his case.

As Constant continues, it becomes clear that the major argument for the claim that religion is a necessary condition for the creation and preservation of a free society is the one mentioned towards the end of the passage quoted above and which has been touched on before: in the nature of political affairs, he claims, liberty will often require the individual to make some sacrifice for it. It is not enough, as he reiterates, to set up paper constitutions, with all sorts of paper guarantees: "Les institutions sont de vaines formes, lorsque nul ne veut se sacrifier pour les institutions."[153] And, as we have seen, he holds that non-compensated self-sacrifice is very difficult to justify on any hedonistic basis.

Once more the full implications of the materialistic and atheistic view of the universe and of man—the vision that had so alarmed him in reading d'Holbach—are exhibited and their supposed necessary effects on human conduct pointed up: "Si la vie n'est, au fond, qu'une apparition bizarre, sans avenir, comme sans passé, et tellement courte qu'on la croirait à peine réelle, à quoi bon s'immoler à des principes dont l'application est au moins éloignée ?"[154] The complete hedonist must accept the logical conclusion of his creed: "L'intérêt bien entendu n'est . . . vu la certitude de la mort, autre chose que la jouissance, combinée, vu la possibilité d'une vie plus ou moins longue, avec la prudence qui donne aux jouissances une certaine durée."[155] Sacrifice for the sake of liberty, Constant is saying, is one form of that ethic of disinterested pursuit of virtue and of ethical perfection that the doctrine of self-interest makes impossible.

Admitting that there have been, historically, strong partisans of liberty who were non- or even anti-religious, Constant attributes their hostility (as will Tocqueville after him) to the fact that religion had been associated with tyrannical governments and that innumerable crimes had been committed in its name.[156] But by virtue of the definition Constant has given to the "sentiment religieux," no incompatibility between *it* and the love of liberty is really possible. The connection of religion and despotism which

---

[153]Ibid., vol. 1, p. xl.

[154]Ibid., vol. 1, pp. 88–89.

[155]*Œuvres*, p. 1618.

[156]*De la religion*, vol. 1, p. xx.

had been manifested so frequently through history must have its source elsewhere, and Constant's theoretical framework has already provided it: "La plupart des reproches qu'on adresse à la religion ne sont mérités que par quelques-uns de ses ministres."[157] While the religious sentiment and love of liberty are perfectly compatible (indeed, as we shall see, he holds that they are more than that), "un élément de nature opposé se glisse quelquefois dans les forms religieuses,"[158] due to the actions of priests. Moreover, Constant even attempts the *tour de force* of applying the historical crimes of religious groups and organizations *against* the Enlightenment philosophy he is attacking, by linking these crimes to the principle of self-interest and to the lack of true religious feeling on the part of the priests. Thus, the opposition to religion of many previous liberals is seen as based on a superficial analysis of the composite nature of religion as it shows itself historically.

The demonstrated willingness of certain anti-religious liberals to sacrifice for their beliefs presents a problem for Constant; the example of the Girondins is one which must have occurred to him in this connection. Constant deals with such cases by asserting that the lovers of liberty were here exhibiting a mode of living on the ethical capital of the past: "leurs vertus mêmes sont des souvenirs d'une autre doctrine. C'est dans leur système une noble inconséquence, c'est un héritage du sentiment religieux. Ils doivent à cet héritage leur force intérieure."[159] The status of this argument is, of course, impossible to assess, since its disproof would require the commission of acts of self-sacrifice on behalf of liberty by men who had been raised in an environment hermetically sealed against inherited religious ideas. In all other cases, the argument of "souvenirs d'une autre doctrine" would be available to Constant as an explanation of their actions.

The distinction between religious sentiment and its institutional forms (often manipulated by priests) serves to generate still another line of argument. Not only does it explain why religion has appeared at times to favor tyranny, but once we have distinguished sentiment from form, we see that the former is consistently *favorable* to freedom.

To some degree, Constant had been anticipated in this connection by David Hume. In his essay, "Of Superstition and Enthusiasm," Hume distinguishes two "corruptions" of "true religion." The first, superstition, he finds to work in favor of the increase of priestly power. (Interestingly, he

[157] Ibid., vol. 1, p. 212.
[158] Ibid., vol. 1, pp. 93–94.
[159] Ibid., vol. 1, pp. 91–92.

here reverses the usual order of causality in eighteenth-century thought, and makes the priestly caste out to be "an invention of a timorous and abject superstition, which, ever diffident of itself, dares not offer up its own devotions.")[160]

More to the point of our concerns, Hume sets forth the proposition that "superstition is an enemy to civil liberty, and enthusiasm a friend to it." The first part of this claim he tries to demonstrate from the fact that superstition is linked to priestly oppression historically; superstition, thus, for Hume, plays a part which writers like d'Holbach ascribed to religion as a whole, in that it "renders men tame and abject, and fits them for slavery."[161] Similarly, he is in agreement with Constant in tying the degenerate form of religion associated with ignorance and despotism to the rule of the priestly caste.

By enthusiasm, on the other hand, Hume seems to mean the sort of direct, often mystical religious experience fostered by groups such as the Anabaptists, Quakers, etc. His description, moreover, shows that his religious "enthusiasm" is not far removed from Constant's "sentiment religieux":

> the imagination swells with great, but confused conceptions, to which no sublunary beauties or enjoyments can correspond. Every thing mortal and perishable vanishes as unworthy of attention; and a full range is given to the fancy in the invisible regions, or world of Spirits, where the soul is at liberty to indulge itself in every imagination which may best suit its present taste and disposition. Hence, arise raptures, transports, and surprising flights of fancy.[162]

Hume associated this form of religious feeling with "bold and ambitious tempers," because of the sense of being God's instrument which private and direct religious experience presumably gives. He notes, historically, the close connection between the sects in England and the Whigs, and between the Tories and the Roman Catholics. The same principle is shown at work in the recent history of France, where "the Jansenists are enthusiasts, and zealous promoters of passionate devotion, and of the inward life ... and [they] preserve alive the small sparks of the love of liberty which are found in the French nation."[163]

[160] David Hume, *On Religion*, ed. by Richard Wollheim (Cleveland, Ohio: Meridian, 1964), pp. 246–248.

[161] Ibid., p. 250.

[162] Ibid., pp. 246–247.

[163] Ibid., pp. 250–251.

Although the germ of this idea thus appears in the writings of Hume, Constant's analysis differs in a number of respects. In the first place, of course, Constant, unlike Hume, does not view the feeling he is describing as pathological, but as of the very essence of religion (an interesting illustration of the difference in temperament between the eighteenth and the early nineteenth centuries). In addition, for him the relation between unspoiled religious emotion and liberty appears to have two aspects. In the first place, the idea of equality tends to follow from the concept which the religious sentiment naturally develops of the relationship between God and men: "Des créatures qui sortent des mains d'un dieu dont la bonté dirige la puissance, étant soumises à la même destinée physique, étant douées des mêmes facultés morales, doivent jouir des mêmes droits."[164]

We may observe this characteristic of religious feeling at work often throughout history. Thus, Constant asserts, at times when the religious sentiment inherent in man bursts through the ossified forms of previous institutionalized religions and founds a new creed, it has been accompanied by a renewed thirst for liberty.[165] Indeed, if we were to take literally the ethical precepts of the major religions, we would find them "toujours d'accord avec les principes de liberté les plus étendus, on pourrait dire, avec des principes de liberté tellement étendus, que jusqu'à ce jour, l'application en a paru impossible dans nos associations politiques."[166] Constant furnishes some examples as historical evidence for the association of liberty and nascent religions (and hence of religious forms when they have emerged fresh from the womb of the religious sentiment):

> les premiers chrétiens ressuscitèrent les nobles doctrines de l'égalité et de la fraternité entre tous les hommes. Rien n'était plus indépendant, nous dirions volontiers plus démocratique, que les Arabes, tant que l'islamisme fut dans sa ferveur. Le protestantisme a préservé l'Allemagne, sous Charles-Quint, de la monarchie universelle. L'Angleterre actuelle lui doit sa constitution.[167]

These historical instances, however, can hardly be said to furnish strong cases in which the early stages of religions promoted liberty. The equality

[164] *De la religion*, vol. 1, pp. 86–87.

[165] In these passages, Constant does not distinguish between religion's promotion of liberty and of equality, for its proclamation of the essential equality of all men before God he thinks implies (in the manner of Locke's *Second Treatise*) the equality of rights.

[166] *De la religion*, vol. 1, p. 84.

[167] Ibid., vol. 1, pp. 87–88.

and fraternity preached by the early Christians was irrelevant, at least directly, to politics: there is no question of opposing slavery or the lack of individual freedom in the ancient world. Constant himself, in discussing the political situaion in antiquity (in connection with the question of the Liberty of the Ancients and of the Moderns), does not think enough of the role of Christianity even to mention it. The equivocation involved in his citation of the Arabs scarcely needs to be made explicit: it is not "independence" or even "democracy" that Constant is discussing, but liberty, and he fails to indicate why he believes the early Arab invaders to have been animated by a love of freedom. The role of Lutheranism in preventing the rise of the sort of monarchy in Germany that the Habsburgs erected in Spain is probably to be ascribed more to its nationalistic bent than to a thirst for liberty on the part of Luther and his followers. Finally, the tendentious quality of Constant's position here is evident from the neglect of any real analysis of the relation of "Protestantism" to the English constitutional struggles of the seventeenth century (Laud was surely as much a Protestant as Pym). In addition, here again, as in the example of Lutheranism and Germany, Constant marks himself as a polemicist by implying that a result favorable to freedom is attributable to the *intention* to promote freedom on the part of certain religious groups and leaders. It would have to be shown that in all these examples, the furtherance of liberty was the *aim* of the movements mentioned, for Constant is using these examples to suggest that early religions manifest a love of liberty, not simply that, due to circumstances, they often work in favor of liberty.

Besides implying the notion of equality, the religious emotion is associated with liberty in another way in Constant's mind:

> le sentiment religieux est une émotion du même genre que toutes nos émotions naturelles ; il est, en conséquence, toujours d'accord avec elles. Il est toujours d'accord avec la sympathie, la pitié, la justice, en un mot, avec toutes les vertus.[168]

The fact that the religious sentiment is an emotion and that sentiments such as justice, sympathy and enthusiasm are (as discussed above) often necessary for the defense of liberty should suggest to the liberal a certain respect for it. With the destructive eighteenth-century rationalists once again in mind, he writes:

[168] Ibid., vol. 1, p. 65.

> Vous ne pouvez porter la cognée à aucune des branches de l'arbre qu'aussitôt le tronc ne soit frappé de mort. Si vous traitez de chimère l'émotion indéfinissable qui semble nous révéler un être infini ... votre dialectique ira plus loin, à votre insu et malgré vous-mêmes. Tout ce qui se passe au fond de notre âme est inexplicable ; et si vous exigez toujours des démonstrations mathématiques, vous n'obtiendrez jamais que des négations. Si le sentiment religieux est une folie, parce que la preuve n'est pas à côté, l'amour est une folie, l'enthousiasme un délire, la sympathie une faiblesse, le dévouement un acte insensé.[169]

The problems with this line of argument appear to be many. In the first place, whether the religious sentiment is in harmony with other "natural emotions" such as sympathy and justice cannot be deduced merely from the fact that all belong to that category (assuming that they do), for there are surely such emotions which conflict: pity and hatred, for instance. Another objection, of which Constant does not even take cognizance, is that love and sympathy differ from the religious sentiment in vital ways: for example, they are not used to establish the existence of a transcendental realm, not available for examination empirically. Thus, one who attacked the religious sentiment from a rationalist point of view would not necessarily be led to attack the sentiments which go to build up the sort of fellow feeling often needed for concerted resistance to tyranny.

There is another way in which religious faith is useful to the preservation of freedom. In this respect, too, Constant anticipates an argument which will be elaborated later by Tocqueville, when he writes: "La philosophie livrée à elle-même, est également sans force : elle conduit au doute, et le doute brise l'énergie de l'âme. Le sentiment religieux peut seul nous sauver."[170] Reason and philosophy in the field of the ultimate questions of meaning and purpose are capable of producing nothing but doubt.[171] But effective action in any field requires a basis of firm conviction. This function of religion is clearly of political significance, for the Hamlet posture is hardly a suitable one in the face of ever-threatening state power. It is not the skeptical attitude, criticizing every position value to shreds, which can

[169] Ibid., vol. 1, pp. xxvii–xxviii.

[170] *De la religion*, vol. 2, p. 484. As early as 1805, he had written in his *Journaux* of "le sentiment religieux, qui est nécessaire ... peut-être à toute espèce de talent." *Œuvres*, p. 476.

[171] *De la religion*, vol. 1, p. 8.

best meet the challenge of the men of power, who know quite well what they are about.

A final service which religious faith performs for liberty would seem to have particular relevance for an age of totalitarianism. Religious belief, Constant asserts, provides a refuge and asylum for those who, true to the ideals of freedom, find themselves for this reason out of tune with their time. A classical example of this is Seneca, living under the despotism of Nero: "pressé par la tyrannie, il se réfugiait où la tyrannie ne pouvait l'atteindre," namely, in the study and cultivation of religious belief.[172] The position of liberty-loving men who find themselves in historical circumstances in which a tyrant has not only gained absolute power, but appears to be supported by virtually everyone, was one which was familiar to Constant: he and Madame de Staël, with a few others, had made her residence at Coppet into a center of anti-Bonapartism in a continent dominated by Napoleon. That such a situation might well again return was a conclusion easy enough for Constant to reach. It is from this viewpoint that we are to understand passages such as the following:

> Lorsque nous voyons s'évanouir nos illusions les plus chéries, la justice, la liberté, la patrie, nous nous flattons qu'il existe quelque part un être qui nous saura gré d'avoir été fidèles, malgré notre siècle, à la justice, à la liberté, à la patrie.[173]

Thus, for Constant, liberty had need of religion above all because the most morally elevated type of individual—the man who will resist tyranny generously when it is directed against others, with firmness and determination when it is directed against himself, and in spite of the moral weakness of the rest of his age—is best nurtured by a religiously-tinged ethic. Religion is not necessary in order for him to discover what his duty is: this is known to him through examination of his own enlightened conscience. But religious faith organizes his ethical life: it provides courage for him to pursue his duty, hope that his activities will bear fruit, and the impulse to go ever further on the road to moral perfection.

[172]Ibid., vol. 1, p. 46, n.
[173]Ibid., vol. 1, p. 9.

Before concluding our examination of Constant's thought, there is a final topic that ought to be discussed: his interpretation of the differences between the "Liberty of the Ancients and of the Moderns."

For nineteenth-century liberalism, the question of the nature of the political organization of classical antiquity had at least two important aspects. In the first place, the Jacobin and Napoleonic periods, by their free use of the rhetoric and of some of the outward political forms of antiquity, had suggested that classical republicanism might be connected with anti-liberal movements. In the second place, for any liberal exploring the connection between freedom and Christianity, the thought and practice of ancient politics becomes immediately relevant, as representing the state of affairs in the Western world before the introduction of Christianity. Particularly, for this second reason, and for the interesting and somewhat unexpected conclusions to which he comes, Constant's ideas on the subject merit examination.

It was by no means due to mere antiquarianism, then, that a number of important liberals in the course of the century turned to the analysis of the ancient republics. Édouard Laboulaye and Fustel de Coulanges in France, the German–American Francis Lieber, Jacob Burckhardt and Lord Acton, all emphasized the essentially illiberal character of the classical republics. The first writer to elaborate the theme in detail, however, is Constant. As will be indicated, the idea underwent important—indeed, for our purposes, crucial—modifications in the thought of the later writers, but the significance of the question was first realized by him.

To become fully aware of what Constant was reacting against, we must turn back to the Enlightenment. That the eighteenth century witnessed something like a renewal of the Renaissance's intense admiration of classical antiquity is widely acknowledged by historians. While in the Germany of Winckelmann, Goethe and Wilhelm von Humboldt, this took the form of devotion to Roman, and especially Greek, models in art and literature, in France particular attention was paid to the ideals and forms of classical politics. If few went the lengths of the oversensitive Madame de Roland, who as a girl wept for not having been born a Roman or a Spartan, the picture of the typical citizen of the ancient republics as austerely virtuous and "natural" was widely accepted by educated persons. Many were led to wonder whether the institutions which had produced this presumably ideal human being could not be reproduced in France with similar beneficent results.

This attitude was characteristic even of some who are famous in the history of liberalism; thus J.-B. Say, in his utopian sketch *Olbie* (1799), argued for the reintroduction of the Roman republican institution of the censor.

The place of this image of antiquity in the rhetoric and actions of the Revolutionary period is well known. As a recent historian of the intellectual background of Jacobinism has said: "The strongest influence on the fathers of totalitarian democracy was that of antiquity, interpreted in their own way."[174] What was of particular concern to the post-Revolutionary liberal was that many had accepted the incessant protestations of love of liberty on the part of the leaders of the Mountain at face value; this in turn had led to a rejection of liberty by all those who were disgusted by the course of French political developments after about 1792. Many people were tempted to conclude that the tyrannical acts of Jacobins and other revolutionary groups were somehow connected with an "excess" of liberty, and resolved that in the future Jacobin tyranny would be avoided by a ruthless suppression of all liberal demands.

Thus the question of the true meaning of ancient liberty was of direct political consequence in Constant's own time. He goes further, however, than merely rectifying a confusion caused by the use of the same term to cover phenomena from two different cultural contexts. He makes it, among other things, the basis of his attack on Rousseau and other thinkers associated with the totalitarian democratic movement of the later eighteenth century.

In his discussion, Constant first poses the question of the meaning of "liberty" to an Englishman, a Frenchman or an American, and finds it in a series of rights: not to be subject to the arbitrary will of an individual or a group of individuals; to speak one's opinion; to choose one's occupation and follow it; to associate with others in the pursuit of common interests; finally, to influence the conduct of government, directly or indirectly. In short, the core of the concept is the existence of a sphere of action reserved for the judgment and will of the individual. Liberty, for the moderns, is an assertion of the individual's *private* life as against his *public* one.

What was understood by "liberty" in the ancient republics is a totally different thing. There, political liberty—a relatively minor part of what is meant by "liberty" in the modern world—formed the core and virtually the whole content of the concept. "Liberty" to the ancients

[174] J. L. Talmon, *The Origins of Totalitarian Democracy* (London: Mercury, 1961), p. 11.

> consistait à exercer collectivement, mais directement, plusieurs parties de la Souveraineté tout entière, à délibérer, sur la place publique, de la guerre et de la paix, à conclure avec les étrangers des traités d'alliance, à voter les lois, à prononcer les jugements, à examiner les comptes, les actes, la gestion des magistrats, à les faire comparaître devant tout le peuple, à les mettre en accusation, à les condamner où à les absoudre.[175]

As far as the sort of liberty dear to the moderns was concerned, however, the ancients ignored it by and large; they considered "comme compatible avec cette liberté collective, l'assujettissement complet de l'individu à l'autorité de l'ensemble."[176] Liberty for them pertained to the public life of the individual, not, as with us, primarily to his private life: "chez les anciens, l'individu, souverain presque habituellement dans les affaires publiques, est esclave dans tous ses rapports privés."[177] In fact, what Constant is describing is the realization of the state presented by Rousseau in the *Contrat social*: "l'aliénation totale de chaque associé avec tous ses droits à toute la communauté . . . la condition est égale pour tous . . . il n'y a pas un associé sur lequel on n'acquière le même droit qu'on lui cède sur soi."[178] The classical polity, so vaunted by certain modern writers, was, in Constant's view, a completely totalitarian state by modern standards.[179]

Constant goes on to outline the reasons for the prevalence of a different sort of liberty in classical times. These are to be found in the fundamental conditions of social life in antiquity. First, the ancient republics were all of small territorial extent. "[P]ar une suite inévitable" of this fact, they are militaristic societies, Constant maintains: they were part of a world where it was constantly a question of conquer or be conquered. Furthermore, such a military way of life necessarily brought with it a society founded on slave labor.[180]

---

[175] *Cours de politiques constitutionnelle*, vol. 2, p. 541.

[176] Ibid.

[177] Ibid., p. 542. Montesquieu had made basically the same point about democracies in general (while refusing to use the term "liberty" to describe them): "Comme dans les démocraties le peuple paraît faire à peu près ce qu'il veut, on a mis la liberté dans ces sortes de gouvernements, et on a confondu le pouvoir du peuple avec la liberté du peuple." *Esprit des lois*, bk. 11, chap. 2.

[178] Jean-Jacques Rousseau, *Du contrat social* (Paris: Garnier, n.d.), bk. 1, chap. 6.

[179] Constant makes a partial exception of Athens, which, in his view, combined both certain totalitarian features (the right of ostracism, for instance) with the most liberal political organization of antiquity. *Œuvres*, pp. 1045–1046.

[180] *Cours de politiques constitutionnelle*, vol. 2, p. 543.

Constant then applies the model of social evolution later to be employed by Comte and especially Herbert Spencer, of the necessary transition from a "military" to a "commercial" society.[181] The period of human history when plunder was the accepted method of obtaining the goods of foreigners gives way to that in which trade gains a grudging recognition: "il doit venir une époque où le commerce remplace la guerre."[182] This has now occurred, and the implications of the fact are of enormous scope.

There were, Constant admits, commercial people in antiquity, but "le commerce était alors un accident heureux : c'est aujourd'hui l'état ordinaire, le but unique, la tendance universelle, la vie véritable des nations."[183] Because of commerce, as well as the progress of knowledge, morals and religion, slavery has disappeared.

Constant then specifies the changes brought about in political life by three basic social changes. In the first place, the large extent of nations today diminishes the importance of each elector. "Le républicain le plus obscure de Rome et de Sparte était une puissance," while this can hardly be said of the citizen of the United States or Great Britain. In modern democracies, the individual citizen can exercise sovereignty only through representatives, which Constant qualifies as sovereignty "d'une manière fictive."[184]

Secondly, the abolition of slavery has eliminated leisure as a way of life for the citizen, and thus removed a necessary condition for the sort of direct democracy prevalent in ancient times. Today, involvement in business affairs requires unceasing attention.

Finally, the commercial way of life tends to create a personality type which values individual independence highly, by demonstrating to people their capacity to fend for themselves, without the need for government supervision and control.[185]

If all these social conditions have made ancient liberty inappropriate to our times, this fact reveals itself in the vast diminution of pleasure which modern man would suffer were he to attempt to live according to the political norms of antiquity. It is highly interesting that Constant puts

---

[181] He thus places himself in the ranks of all the social thinkers of the nineteenth century —including Saint-Simon, Durkheim, Spencer, Maine, Tönnies, etc.—who conceived of a dichotomous division of social evolution.

[182] *Cours de politiques constitutionnelle*, vol. 2, p. 544.

[183] Ibid.

[184] *Œuvres*, p. 1046.

[185] *Cours de politiques constitutionnelle*, vol. 2, p. 546.

the issue between ancient and modern liberty in the form of a hedonistic calculation. For the ancients, "l'exercice des droits de cité constituait l'occupation, et pour ainsi dire, l'amusement de tous ... la volonté de chacun avait une influence réelle ; l'exercice de cette volonté [était] un plaisir vif et répété." This is the sort of pleasure with which the enjoyment generated by participation in elections for legislative representatives cannot compare. In fact, given slavery, unless the citizen did apply himself to politics, he would suffer perpetual boredom, since due to the stage of social development achieved, other pleasures were quite scarce. But today the commercial spirit has enormously increased the possibilities of enjoyment outside of public life, and personal independence today is the chief precondition for happiness. Constant poses a hedonistic calculus in these terms:

> Les anciens trouvaient plus de jouissances dans leur existence publique, et ils en trouvaient moins dans leur existence privée : en conséquence, lorsqu'ils sacrifiaient la liberté individuelle à la liberté politique, ils sacrifiaient moins pour obtenir plus ... En imitant les anciens, les modernes sacrifieraient donc plus pour obtenir moins.[186]

It was this fundamental fact, traceable to greatly changed social conditions, that the leaders of the Jacobin party refused to see. They had been taught by Rousseau and Mably to strive for liberty as the austere and virtuous citizens of Sparta and Rome understood the term. They found that French society as a whole resisted; they were forced to use extraordinary means to impose their Republic of Virtue: terror as an acknowledged, even glorified instrument of government, was the result. Like their teachers, Robespierre and Saint-Just took not the slightest notice of the alterations in character and personality produced by two thousand years of social evolution. It was in vain that they denounced and blamed dark conspiracies and the machinations of English spies: what they were combating was the *Zeitgeist*, and of necessity they went down to defeat.

Of great interest in Constant's discussion of this theme, both in *De l'esprit de conquête* and in his talk to the Athénée Royal in 1819, is the fact that it is completely *wertfrei*. In neither case does he ever criticize the ancients for their political arrangements, which, from his liberal point of

[186] *Œuvres*, pp. 1046–1047. Michel's remark on this is worth noting: "Observation subtile et profonde, mais qui fait reposer, en dernière analyse, l'individualisme sur un calcul d'intérêt." Op. cit., p. 312.

view, had to seem totalitarian.[187] Indeed, he goes out of his way to emphasize his great admiration for the quality of mind and character produced by the ancient commonwealths: it is with a certain sadness that he notes that they seem almost to be of a different nature from our own, "tellement forts de leurs propres forces, avec un tel sentiment d'énergie et de dignité." Modern republics, such as Switzerland and Holland, are in contrast "moins brillantes et plus paisibles," and have favored commerce at the expense of the virtues cultivated in older days.[188] In fact, in the first version of the theme, in 1813, Constant takes the opportunity to express his idea of the inferiority of men under advanced civilization, with their lack of enthusiasm and strong convictions, their morbid penchant for self-observation, etc.[189] His refusal to condemn the ancients for their political organization is manifested particularly in the fact that he never questions that the term "liberty" may validly be used to refer to their conception: indeed, the initial purpose of his lecture was to illustrate the differences in meaning between the term in different cultural contexts, and he does this in as perfectly a detached spirit as any cultural relativist could wish. But dear as the classical republic must seem to any person who values a highly developed form of humanity, there is no hope that it can be resurrected. The ancients lived under a given social system, which *necessarily* preceded ours, and "leur organisation sociale les conduisait à désirer une liberté toute différente" from the modern variety; while, in the present day, "citoyens des républiques, sujets des monarchies, tous veulent des jouissances, et nul ne peut, dans l'état actuel des sociétés, ne pas en vouloir."[190] For Constant, it is not a question of choice between the older and newer conceptions of freedom:

> nous ne pouvons plus jouir de la liberté des anciens.... Notre liberté, à nous, doit se composer de la jouissance paisible de l'indépendance privée.... Puisque nous vivons dans les temps modernes, je veux la liberté convenable aux temps modernes .[191]

[187] In a similar vein, Tocqueville, at the end of the second volume of *Democracy*, asserts that it is ultimately impossible to pass judgment on the relative merits of aristocratic and democratic man. *Democracy in America*, trans. by Henry Reeve (New York: Vintage, 1954), vol. 2, p. 351. This is only one noteworthy example of the impact on two such prominent liberals as Constant and Tocqueville of the historicist movement.

[188] *Œuvres*, pp. 1027–1028.

[189] Ibid., p. 1047.

[190] Ibid., p. 1047, n.

[191] *Cours de politique constitutionnelle*, vol. 2, p. 547.

What is most interesting from our point of view, however, is what Constant *omits* from his analysis: nowhere in his discussion of the problem of the liberty of the ancients *versus* that of the moderns does he so much as mention Christianity, and he makes no references to it as being involved in the changeover from the classical to the modern concepts. Although elsewhere he speaks of "l'Évangile, doctrine céleste qui a rendu à l'homme sa liberté légitime et sa dignité première,"[192] there is no attempt at all to develop an analysis showing how the Gospels might have been influential in creating modern liberty. Thus, the following statement by one of Constant's recent interpreters is difficult to understand:

> Suchte Constant das Wesen der modernen Freiheit mit Hilfe des Vergleiches mit dem antiken Freiheitsbegriff zu charakterisieren, so stellte sich ihm damit zugleich die Frage, worauf denn der tiefgreifende Wandel des Verhältnisses des Einzelnen zum Staat seit der Antike letztlich zurückzuführen sei. *Es war dies für ihn die Leistung der christlichen Religion.* Diese habe gleichsam den Ring aufgesprengt, mit dem der antike Staat den Einzelnen in den Bereich seiner eigenen Ziele einschnürte, indem sie die menschliche Existenz im Transzendenten begründete und dem einzelnen neben der Bindung an das Gemeinwesen eine Bindung an ewige Normen, an die Gesetze einer göttlichen Weltordnung erlegte.[193]

The only problem with this is that it bears no resemblance at all to anything Constant wrote in comparing the liberty of the ancients and the moderns.[194]

A number of the liberal writers who followed him, however, did place Christianity in the forefront of the sources of the modern conception of freedom.[195] We may take as an example of this tendency Constant's disciple, Édouard Laboulaye, who, in an essay written in 1863, takes up the

---

[192] *De la religion*, vol. 3, p. 233.

[193] Gall, op. cit., p. 117. (Italics added.)

[194] Despite the thoroughness of Gall's book, and despite many interesting insights of his, this is only one example where he has overemphasized the religious background and orientation of Constant's thought. On the point at issue here, a writer such as Michel adheres to the clear meaning of the text in contrasting Constant's silence on the role of Christianity with Laboulaye's, placing it at the center of his discussion. Michel, op. cit., p. 313.

[195] Numa Denis Fustel de Coulanges, *The Ancient City* (New York: Anchor, 1956), pp. 389–396; Francis Lieber, *On Civil Liberty and Self-Government* (Philadelphia: Lippincott, 1859), pp. 50–51.

theme Constant had dealt with.[196] He follows his master in his description of both ancient and modern liberty, but when he turns to discussing the reasons for the transformation of the first into the second, he departs from Constant completely. There is no mention of underlying social condition. Instead, he asserts:

> Si Jésus-Christ n'avait point paru sur la terre, j'ignore comment le monde aurait résisté à ce despotisme qui l'étouffait ... en politique, aussi bien qu'en morale et philosophie, l'Évangile a renouvelé les âmes.[197]

Laboulaye concedes that at first glance the teachings of Jesus appear to ignore politics entirely, having reference to a different order of concerns. But, as with Lord Acton in dealing with the same question, supreme importance is attributed to the passage in which Jesus declares: "Render unto God the things that are God's." Of this, Laboulaye asserts:

> il proclame un principe nouveau en contradiction avec toutes les idées antiques.... Proclamer que Dieu a des droits, c'est déchirer l'unité du despotisme. Là est le germe de la révolution qui sépare le monde ancien du monde moderne.[198]

He points out that Rousseau well understood the role that Christianity had played in this connection, and had regretted it bitterly.[199]

How Laboulaye conceives this process to have taken place is very roughly sketched. From the fact that one is enjoined to respect the rights of God, it follows that the individual now had *duties* independent of the state. But a *duty* to perform a certain action implies the moral *right* to perform that action: "il y a des devoirs, et par conséquent des droits pour l'âme immortelle, droits et devoirs indépendants de l'État, sur lesquels le prince n'a point d'autorité. La conscience est affranchie, l'individu existe."[200] Furthermore,

[196]"La liberté antique et la liberté moderne," in *L'état et ses limites* (Paris: Charpentier, 1865), pp. 103–137.

[197]Ibid., p. 109.

[198]Ibid., p. 110.

[199]Ibid. Rousseau states: "Jésus vint établir sur la terre un royaume spirituel : ce qui, séparant le système théologique du système politique, fit que l'État cessa d'être un, et causa les divisions intestines qui n'ont jamais cessé d'agiter les peuples chrétiens." *Du contrat social*, bk. 4, chap. 8.

[200]Laboulaye, op. cit., pp. 110–111. This, as will later become apparent, resembles to a certain extent Lord Acton's own rationale for liberty, but not his conception of the *historical development* by which liberty had to some extent been realized.

Christianity includes an ethic touching on every part of life; thus, all interpersonal relations are brought under the heading of "things that are God's," and freed from state control. Laboulaye even asserts that included in this pristine Christian conception is the reduction of "le rôle de l'État à une mission de justice et de paix"—in other words, the nineteenth-century liberal *Nachtwächterstaat*![201]

Basically, Laboulaye treats the question of historical causation here in a journalistic rather than a philosophical manner. For him, it is sufficient to draw from a Biblical passage a certain conclusion to have adequately demonstrated why certain political norms prevailed at one time and not at another. The closest he comes to explaining how the idea allegedly contained in Jesus's admonition was translated into social reality is in discussing the early Christian martyrs: "C'est à cette sainteté que nous devons la liberté moderne. Il y a là des souvenirs que rien ne peut effacer.... Quand une idée est vraie, elle s'empare des âmes, et finit toujours par triompher."[202] The difference between this sort of analysis and that offered by Constant (and, as we shall see, by Acton) hardly requires underscoring.

---

[201] Ibid., p. 111.
[202] Ibid., p. 115.

CHAPTER 2

Alexis de Tocqueville

For most of the great social thinkers of the nineteenth century, the changes in European society associated with the Industrial Revolution and the political upheavals of the modern age (including especially the French Revolution) were by no means isolated phenomena. Rather, they tended to see them as part of a much grander development, of whose continuing advance they themselves were living witnesses.[1] This is particularly true of Alexis de Tocqueville; from the beginning of his writing career to the end, he was profoundly aware of the fact that, as he puts it in *Democracy in America*, "the great revolution by which [modern society] has been created is not yet over."[2] In his last great work, *The Old Régime and the French Revolution*, he repeats the idea, stating that "the Revolution is still operative." [3]

What this Revolution consisted of in Tocqueville's conception was largely a "progressive decay of the institution stemming from the Middle Ages";[4] to employ terms which sociologists have since made familiar, what

[1]Robert A. Nisbet, *The Sociological Tradition* (New York: Basic Books, 1966), pp. 21–44.

[2]*Democracy in America*, vol. 2, p. 349.

[3]Alexis de Tocqueville, *The Old Régime and the French Revolution*, trans. by Stuart Gilbert (Garden City, N.Y.: Anchor, 1955), p. 20.

[4]Ibid., p. 16. He refers to the mid-eighteenth century as "that generation which had

Tocqueville saw was an ongoing replacement of the relationships, values, sentiments and ideas associated with *Gemeinschaft*, by those pertaining to *Gesellschaft*. Within the family, between landowners and their tenants, masters and servants, among those in the same profession, and between subjects and rulers, the old ways of traditional European society were giving way to new ones, loosening group ties and emphasizing the individual's reason, well-being and will.[5] At the center of this Revolution, Tocqueville placed the concept of *democracy*.

In a few famous lines in the introduction to the first volume of *Democracy in America*, Tocqueville traced the great transition which had, since about the turn of the millennium, brought to the fore the principle of equality, and now seemed to be preparing its complete victory. With "a kind of religious awe," he discerns the will of God in this seemingly inevitable historical evolution:

> The gradual development of the principle of equality is, therefore, a providential fact. It has all the chief characteristics of such a fact: it is universal, it is lasting, it constantly eludes all human interference, and all events as well as all men contribute to its progress.[6]

Five years later, he repeats this view: "I am firmly convinced that the democratic revolution which we are now beholding is an irresistible fact, against which it would be neither desirable nor prudent to contend," and adds that he intends to concentrate mainly on pointing out the dangers of this process and how they might best be avoided.[7] It is in fact against this background of an inevitable trend towards democracy that Tocqueville seeks to make a place for the values which were closest to his heart. "No man can struggle with advantage against the spirit of his age and country,"[8] he wrote; but it was his hope that with knowledge, intelligence and spirit, the statesman and even the political philosopher can exert sufficient influence to make a difference.

---

decisively broken with the Middle Ages." Alexis de Tocqueville, *"The European Revolution" and Correspondence with Gobineau*, trans. and ed. by John Lukacs (Garden City, N.Y.: Anchor, 1959), p. 190.

[5] *Democracy in America*, vol. 2, pp. 192, 196–198.

[6] Ibid., vol. 1, p. 6.

[7] Ibid., vol. 2, p. vi.

[8] Ibid., vol. 2, p. 269.

What then were these values for which Tocqueville struggled? There is little need to emphasize that among the highest of these was liberty. "Freedom is, in truth, a *sacred* thing,"[9] he asserted; and, on another occasion, he wrote, "I regard, as I have always done, liberty as the greatest of all goods."[10] Towards the end of his life, in a touching passage in *The Old Régime*, he speaks of the love of liberty which noble spirits experience: "ils la considèrent elle-même comme un bien si précieux et si nécessaire qu'aucun autre ne pourrait les consoler de sa perte et qu'ils se consolent de tout en la goûtant."[11] Freedom in the negative sense, the "liberty of the moderns" of which Constant wrote, which consists in the absence of coercion, was a principal value of Tocqueville's.

Often, however, Tocqueville also uses the term "liberty" in the sense of the right to participate in political decision-making, generally on the local level. For example, in his chapter on "Why Democratic Nations Show a More Ardent and Enduring Love of Equality Than of Liberty," in the second volume of *Democracy in America*, the sort of liberty that is referred to is this kind of *political* liberty.[12] This comes out most sharply, perhaps, in the foreword to *The Old Régime*. There, in discussing the evils which beset modern democratic society, he states, "Freedom and freedom alone can extirpate these vices. For only freedom can deliver the members of a community from that isolation which is the lot of the individual left to his own devices, and *compelling* [*contraindre*] them to get in touch with each other, promote an active sense of fellowship."[13] Here he is writing of political liberty, and the irony of using the term "liberty" in connection with compelling a more intense association among men appears to escape him. We will touch later on certain problems raised by Tocqueville's exaltation of political participation; here I wish only to suggest that it represents a verbal connecting link, as it were, between liberty in the negative sense and his other controlling value, the realization of a certain sort of human personality.

[9]Jack Lively, *The Social and Political Thought of Alexis de Tocqueville* (Oxford: Clarendon, 1965), p. 8.

[10]Ibid., p. 20.

[11]Alexis de Tocqueville, *Œuvres Complètes*, ed. by J.-P. Mayer (Paris: Gallimard, 1952), vol. 2, pp. i, 217.

[12]*Democracy in America*, vol. 2, pp. 99–103.

[13]*Old Régime*, p. xiv. (Italics added.)

No-one who has read the works of Tocqueville can fail to perceive that a profound admiration for energetic, passionate and heroic characters breaks through again and again. "I rejoice in finding [people] praiseworthy," he wrote Gobineau, "and nothing is so delightful to me as are sentiments of admiration when they seem warranted."[14] What particularly evoked his admiration was the spectacle of grandeur in human character and action. He admits that he has been concerned, in his discussion of eighteenth-century France, to "throw into relief" virtues such as "a healthy independence, high ambitions, faith in oneself and in a cause" wherever he found them.[15] Later he speaks with evident feeling of many of the men of that era:

> this spirit of independence kept alive in many individuals their sense of personality and encouraged them to retain their color and relief. More than this, it fostered a healthy self-respect and often an overmastering desire to make a name for themselves. This is why we find in eighteenth-century France so many outstanding personalities, those men of genius, proud and greatly daring, who made the Revolution what it was: at once the admiration and the terror of succeeding generations.[16]

The same almost Renaissance respect for energy and force, largely irrespective of the end aimed at (so long as it was of great scope),[17] is shown in response to Gobineau's suggestion that France was a nation in decline: Tocqueville asks whether it had not "produced a constant stream of great writers during the past three centuries, stirring and moving the spirit of mankind most powerfully—whether in the right or wrong direction may be arguable, but their power one cannot doubt."[18]

This appears to be above all the sense in which Tocqueville was an aristocrat in politics. It is not difficult to see a picture of himself in his description of the aristocratic posture:

---

[14] *European Revolution*, p. 324.

[15] *Old Régime*, p. xii.

[16] Ibid., p. 120.

[17] This is not to imply that Tocqueville would have approved of these qualities in the service of what he recognized to be criminal ends—he does not appear to have had much admiration for a Marat or a Robespierre. But such virtues, when displayed by persons of a wide range of attitudes and aims, have an intrinsic value, he thought.

[18] *European Revolution*, p. 325.

> Aristocracies often commit very tyrannical and inhuman actions, but they rarely entertain grovelling thoughts; and they show a kind of haughty contempt of little pleasures, even while they indulge in them. The effect is to raise greatly the general pitch of society. In aristocratic ages vast ideas are commonly entertained of the dignity, the power, and the greatness of man.[19]

This aspect of Tocqueville's thought is linked to a number of his recurrent preoccupations, for instance, his emphasis on the need to arouse pride in modern-day man, and relatedly, his horror of all theories which suggest that man is a helpless pawn in the hands of fate (this comes out most strongly, of course, in his dispute with Gobineau on racism). Here, I would like to indicate its manifestation in another, less appealing area of his thinking, and one which has only recently begun to receive the attention it ought to have: Tocqueville's commitment to the imperialism of the European nations and his admiration of war.[20] Since they are relatively unexamined aspects of his thought, a somewhat extended discussion will be necessary to put them in proper perspective.

As far as imperialism is concerned, we should note that, practically, Tocqueville worked for the French government in connection with its pacification of Algeria. Theoretically, he went even beyond his friend Beaumont's attitude, expressed in the latter's book on Ireland: "What is an empire which consents to dismember itself? Is it not a power in decline which diminishes in extent, or does it not, in an event, appear to be?"[21] Tocqueville believed positively in the value of empire, for its civilizing work, but more for the sake of the imperial power. While Nassau Senior, representative of the Little England position, wrote Tocqueville that it was

---

[19] *Democracy in America*, vol. 2, p. 45. That Tocqueville shared the caste feelings of the nobleman is unquestionable. Nassau Senior reports on a conversation with him in 1849, in which Tocqueville refers to the "freemasonry" existing among aristocrats: "When I talk to a gentilhomme, though we have not two ideas in common, though all his opinions, wishes and thoughts are opposed to mine, yet I feel at once that we belong to the same family, that we speak the same language, that we understand one another. I may like a bourgeois better, but he is a stranger." M. C. M. Simpson, ed., *Correspondence and Conversation of Alexis de Tocqueville with Nassau William Senior from 1834 to 1859* (London: King, 1872), vol. 1, p. 69.

[20] Melvin Richter has dealt with the former in "Tocqueville and Algeria," *The Review of Politics* 25 (July 1963), pp. 362–398. The subject is also discussed in Seymour Drescher, *Tocqueville and England* (Cambridge, Mass.: Harvard University Press, 1964).

[21] Quoted in Drescher, op. cit., p. 114.

his view that "India is and always has been a great misfortune to us; and, that if it were possible to get quit of it, we should be richer and stronger,"[22] and much of English liberal opinion shared his view, Tocqueville was of a different position. The writer who had traced the discovery and settlement of the American continent by a free people found it possible to write to an English friend as follows:

> There has never been anything under the sun as extraordinary as the conquest, and above all the government of India by the English, anything which from every corner of the globe more attracts the imagination of men to that small island of whose very name the Greeks were unaware. Do you believe, madame, that a people can, after having filled this immense space in the imagination of the human species, withdraw from it with impunity?[23]

To Gobineau, Tocqueville confided that he saw European imperialism as another manifestation of God's will; nations which had been savage hordes only a few centuries before have now undertaken the domination of the globe; he adds, characteristically, that they "are often the greatest rogues, but at least they are rogues to whom God gave will and power."[24] When, in *Democracy*, he speaks of the nations which, through their conception and carrying out of vast designs have altered the course of history, those he mentions are the imperial peoples *par excellence*, the Romans and the English.[25]

Even more surprising, perhaps, than Tocqueville's enthusiasm for imperialist ventures is his defense of war as a valuable social institution. His belligerent attitude during the "Eastern Crisis" of 1840 earned him the censures of his friends, Senior and John Stuart Mill,[26] and the pacifism of the July Monarchy was one of the bourgeois traits he held against it. But Mill really had little reason to be surprised, having reviewed and presumably carefully read both volumes of the *Democracy*. In the second volume, after discussing the factors which made for less frequent wars under the conditions of modern society, Tocqueville states:

---

[22] Simpson, op. cit., vol. 2, p. 214.

[23] Quoted in Drescher, op. cit., p. 182.

[24] *European Revolution*, pp. 267–268.

[25] *Democracy in America*, vol. 1, p. 245. It is significant that he explains this by citing the fact that they were governed by aristocratic institutions.

[26] Drescher, op. cit., pp. 159–160.

> I do not wish to speak ill of war: war almost always enlarges the mind of a people and raises its character. In some cases it is the only check to the excessive growth of certain propensities that naturally spring out of the equality of conditions, and it must be considered as a necessary corrective to certain inveterate diseases to which democratic communities are liable. War has great advantages.[27]

Here Tocqueville is joining the ranks of other non-utilitarian liberals, whose love of individuality per se and of effective and energetic personalities was also sometimes so great as to lead them to mourn the seeming disappearance of war from the central place it had filled in European history in modern times. Wilhelm von Humboldt furnished a good example of this tendency when he wrote, towards the end of the eighteenth century:

> Ist mir der Krieg eine der heilsamsten Erscheinungen zur Bildung des Menschengeschlechts, und ungern seh' ich ihn nach und nach immer mehr vom Schauplatz zurücktreten.[28]

This is closely linked to Humboldt's disdain for the small-minded preference for pleasure over greatness of character and achievement. Rather naively he asserts: "Gewiss ist noch kein Mensch tief genug gesunken, um für sich selbst Wohlstand und Glück der Grösse vorzuziehen."[29] The connection between these two positions is clear enough: war is the least self-indulgent and hedonistic of activities (at least when waged by relatively prosperous modern societies, which do not primarily engage in war for reasons of plunder; the taking of booty by modern armies is also very incidental to their main purpose), and while it develops the personality by promoting such virtues as comradeship, the sense of personal honor, etc., it represents above all the ultimate in self-sacrifice for the soldier. For this reason war was able to exert a certain appeal on those among the liberals who feared that hedonism was a danger to their ideal of personality; this was the case, for instance, with Benjamin Constant.[30]

---

[27] *Democracy in America*, vol. 2, p. 283.

[28] Wilhelm von Humboldt, *Werke*, ed. by Andress Flitner and Klaus Giel (Darmstadt: Wissenschaftliche Buchgesellschaft, 1960), vol. 1, p. 98.

[29] Ibid., p. 72. It is no accident that the author of these words was the one minister at the Congress of Vienna who rejoiced at the news that Napoleon had returned from Elba, because "now we shall have some life." Juliette Bauer, *Lives of the Brothers Humboldt* (New York: Harper, 1853), p. 351.

[30] See, for instance, the comment: "Je reconnais volontiers [war's] avantages.... A de

But neither Humboldt nor Constant went as far as Tocqueville did when he termed war a "necessary corrective." Constant, in fact, explicitly asserts that the advantages of war pertain to particular stages of social evolution, which have now been superseded.[31] It is otherwise with Tocqueville. Here, even more clearly than in the case of imperialism, we see that he is following out the implications of his commitment to energy, grandeur and passion as values independent of liberty. For he is under no illusions as to the problems created for a liberal society by engaging in war:

> The democratic tendency that leads men unceasingly to multiply the privileges of the state and to circumscribe the right of private persons is much more rapid and constant among those nations that are exposed by their position to great and frequent wars than among all others.[32]

What we have in the deliberate promotion of occasional wars is an instance of what Tocqueville suggests the statesman should look upon as one of his tasks. Considering that that which "is most to be dreaded is that in the midst of the small, incessant occupations of private life, ambition should lose its vigor and its greatness; that the passions of man should abate, but at the same time be lowered; so that the march of society should every day become more tranquil and less aspiring," Tocqueville proposes the following:

> I think, then, that the leaders of modern society would be wrong to seek to lull the community by a state of too uniform and too peaceful happiness, and that it is well to expose it from time to time to matters of difficulty and danger in order to raise ambition and to give it a field of action.[33]

Here there is no suggestion that the purpose in exposing the community to difficulty and danger is to better maintain liberty; passionate and vigorous action are considered goods in themselves, deserving of cultivation by the political authorities.

---

certaines époques de l'espèce humaine, elle est dans la nature de l'homme. Elle favorise alors le développement de ses plus belles et de ses plus grandes facultés," etc. *Œuvres*, p. 991.

[31] Ibid.

[32] *Democracy in America*, vol. 2, p. 318.

[33] Ibid., vol. 2, p. 261.

Thus, in considering Tocqueville's profound wish to secure a place for religion in the modern world, we must be aware that freedom alone is not always what is on his mind; that sometimes, at least, he is willing to sacrifice it to his aesthetic ideal of human personality. Tocqueville writes not simply as a liberal, but, as he himself put it (but with a different meaning): "a liberal of a new kind."

But, whether or not he was a liberal of a new kind, Tocqueville shared a number of the basic ideas of earlier nineteenth-century liberalism. Near, if not at, the center of the political problem is how government may be limited;[34] for the tendency of the state to increase its power is so clearly attested to by history that it may be regarded "in the nature of all governments to seek constantly to enlarge their sphere of action";[35] it is an "instinctive desire" on their part.[36]

In *Democracy*, Tocqueville dates the great increase of centralization and government regulation "everywhere" from about the outbreak of the French Revolution;[37] as far as France was concerned, however, it is a much older phenomenon, dating from the time of Philip the Fair.[38] Part of the great achievement of his work on the *Old Régime*, of course, was to show the extent to which there existed continuity between the policy and guiding principles of French monarchy and those of the French Revolution (with the exception of a brief period under the National Assembly) and, especially, Napoleon. Already by the eighteenth century in France the government had become a sort of "Divine Providence";[39] both in regard to local institutions and authorities, and in connection with the private

[34] By "government" and "state," we must understand the *central government*. Tocqueville often writes in the spirit of the Tenth Amendment to the United States Constitution; that is, he separates out the powers of the central government on the one hand, and those of the local authorities and the people on the other. This is connected with his tendency to use "freedom" sometimes to designate participation in political decision-making by the citizens.

[35] *Democracy in America*, vol. 2, p. 311.

[36] *Old Régime*, p. 58.

[37] *Democracy in America*, vol. 2, p. 331.

[38] Ibid., vol. 2, p. 371. Why, in that case, it does not begin to assume the characteristics of a "providential fact," to which we must bow, is unclear.

[39] *Old Régime*, p. 70.

individual, it played "the part of an indefatigable mentor" and kept "the nation in quasi-paternal tutelage."[40]

This is a development which has continued into the nineteenth century; it has been promoted by reactionaries as well as revolutionaries. Just as there was reason for Louis XVI to rejoice at much of the work of the Constituent Assembly in demolishing the old immediate powers in France,[41] the monarchs who combined against the Revolution nevertheless learned much from it, and in many respects, in the period in which Tocqueville wrote, were copying its methods.[42]

In general, the process by which the aristocracy and aristocratic institutions were decaying or being suppressed led automatically to an increase in state power. In a democratic society, there exist only individuals and the state, and, everyone having been rendered isolated and equally helpless (or nearly so), it is natural that the central power finds its authority increasing. In fields such as charity, education, religious life, supervision of industry, government in modern society is taking on more and more functions, as groups which had previously been active decline and disappear.[43] This tendency is the normal one for democracies:

> a democratic government increases its power simply by the fact of its permanence. Time is on its side . . . in the democratic ages which are opening upon us, individual independence and local liberties will ever be the products of art . . . centralization will be the natural government.[44]

What this meant concretely Tocqueville clearly understood. The state for him was no metaphysical "coldest of all cold monsters": rather, the increase of state power meant the increase in the authority of a particular class, the bureaucracy. Already before the Revolution they had in France formed a grouping with every mark of a distinct class:

---

[40] Ibid., p. 41; see also pp. 51 and 198.

[41] Tocqueville quotes with great effect a secret letter from Mirabeau to the king, praising the Revolution for (so far) having accomplished much in concentrating power in the hands of the monarchy; much of what it had done "would have pleased Richelieu." Ibid., p. 8.

[42] Ibid., pp. 8–9.

[43] *Democracy in America*, vol. 2, pp. 321–324.

[44] Ibid., vol. 2, pp. 312, n., 313.

> Les fonctionnaires administratifs, presque tous bourgeois, forment déjà une classe qui a son esprit particulier, ses traditions, ses vertus, son honneur, son orgueil propre. C'est l'aristocratie de la société nouvelle.[45]

The ideal of the future for most Frenchmen, he asserts, had become one in which "an all-powerful bureaucracy not only took charge of affairs of State but controlled men's private lives."[46]

This tendency for the bureaucracy to gather all of society's life and power into its own hands was not limited to France. It is part of the growing statism which characterizes the emerging triumph of democracy:

> In proportion as the functions of the central power are augmented, the number of public officers by whom that power is represented must increase also. They form a nation within each nation; and as they share the stability of the government, they more and more fill up the place of an aristocracy. In almost every part of Europe the government rules in two ways: it rules one portion of the citizens by the fear which they feel for its agents, and the other by the hope they have of becoming its agents.[47]

What was occurring in Europe, Tocqueville thought, was that the powers of the central government were becoming more absolute and more extensive, and the people becoming insensibly the servants of the administration, frightened of incurring the displeasure of the obscurest government clerk. Finally, summing up this development, Tocqueville presents, at the conclusion of the second volume of *Democracy*, his picture of the "Sort of Despotism Democratic Nationals Have to Fear," of mankind being watched over by "an immense and tutelary power, which takes upon itself alone to secure their gratifications and to watch over their fate."[48]

---

[45] *Œuvres completes*, vol. 2, pp. ii, 132.

[46] *Old Régime*, p. 167.

[47] *Democracy in America*, vol. 2, p. 323, n. The degree to which place-hunting was a mania among the French and other continental nations was a problem for Tocqueville. It aroused his contempt, as well as his fears for the effects on national character. See, e.g., ibid., vol. 2, p. 263; *Old Régime*, p. 91.

[48] *Democracy in America*, vol. 2, p. 336.

Tocqueville accepts Constant's view that the danger of despotic government is closely associated with the growth of materialism and hedonism in modern society.[49] This phenomenon was one of the most striking which Tocqueville encountered in the United States, and he linked it to the rising influence of *bourgeois* ways and values throughout society:

> The effort to satisfy even the least wants of the body and to provide the little conveniences of life is uppermost in every mind [in the United States]. . . . The passion for physical comforts is essentially a passion of the middle classes; with those classes it grows and spreads, with them it is preponderant. From them it mounts into the higher orders of society and descends into the mass of the people.[50]

A much more accurate prophet than Marx, Tocqueville saw that the future would not bring an accentuated polarization of classes, but rather a *Verbürgerlichung* of all classes, with the industrial and mercantile classes calling the tune for the rest of society. That this had occurred in the United States impressed itself forcefully on Tocqueville's mind during his stay there: in America he had seen a whole people who had given themselves over utterly to business. He compared the Americans to a joint-stock company which had been "placed in the midst of a new and boundless country, which their principal object is to explore for purposes of profit,"[51] and termed them "the most grasping nation on the globe."[52]

The results of this *bourgeois* mentality penetrating all of society are manifold. In the first place, there is in this sort of life a brutishness that provokes Tocqueville's disgust. In *Democracy* we hear the *cri de cœur* of an aristocrat who sees the likely man of the future before him: "nothing conceivable is so petty, so insipid, so crowded with paltry interests—in a word, so anti-poetic—as the life of a man in the United States."[53] He

---

[49] Tocqueville does not refer to the ideas of Constant in regard to this problem, nor does he mention him at all in any of his major works, to my knowledge. But he can hardly have avoided reading such works as *De l'esprit de conquête*, by the leading French liberal of the generation preceding his.

[50] *Democracy in America*, vol. 2, pp. 136–137. Besides wealth as a source of creature comforts, Tocqueville finds that it is valued also as the last remaining creator of status distinction in democratic societies. Ibid., vol. 2, pp. 239–240. This is a factor that Constant seems not to have considered.

[51] Ibid., vol. 2, pp. 247–248.

[52] Ibid., vol. 1, p. 360.

[53] Ibid., vol. 2, p. 78.

foresees the slow death of what aristocratic ages had conceived of as the truly human ideal:

> to [the enjoyment of pleasures] the heart, the imagination, and life itself are unreservedly given up, till, in snatching at these lesser gifts, men lose sight of those more precious possessions which constitute the glory and greatness of mankind.[54]

Tocqueville hastens to add that he is not suggesting that this will lead to transgressing the law or the moral code; rather, it is wholly legitimate pleasures which are the danger:

> By these means a kind of virtuous materialism may ultimately be established in the world, which would not corrupt, but enervate, the soul, and noiselessly unbend the spring of action.[55]

This tendency of democratic ages is so pronounced that it is visible even in intellectual areas: a sort of intellectual hedonism gains ground, with men desiring to obtain high returns with little effort, and therefore slothfully having recourse to the relatively imprecise "general ideas."[56]

Thus, the striving for material gratifications which is characteristic of democratic times violates Tocqueville's ideal of man, and he experiences the same sort of despair that Max Weber did in foreseeing the future world peopled by "specialists without spirit, sensualists without heart."[57] The mischief goes even beyond blatantly violating the ideal human personality that Tocqueville held dear, however. For the ramifications of this new value system extend into the political realm, and endanger also the preservation of the liberal society itself.

It is in this connection that we encounter a concept which is central to Tocqueville's prognosis of the coming crisis of society: that of "individualism." As was customary in his time, he used the term in a pejorative

---

[54] Ibid., vol. 2, p. 141.

[55] Ibid. In another place, however, Tocqueville seems to accept the modern taste for well-being: "Man cannot be cured of the love of riches, but they may be persuaded to enrich themselves by none but honest means." Ibid., vol. 2, p. 27. It is here, he asserts, that the role of religion is to be found.

[56] Ibid., vol. 2, p. 18.

[57] Max Weber, *The Protestant Ethic and the Spirit of Capitalism* (New York: Scribner, 1958), p. 182.

sense.[58] For him, individualism was the counterpart of the "Cartesian" tendency of the democratic man to trust to his own mind solely, ignoring traditional hierarchies of intellectual authority. In the democratic period,

> all [man's] feelings are turned towards himself alone. … Individualism is a mature and calm feeling, which disposes each member of the community to sever himself from the mass of his fellows and to draw apart with his family and his friends, so that after he has thus formed a little circle of his own, he willingly leaves society at large to itself.[59]

The underlying cause of this new frame of mind is the progressive decay of the social structure inherited from the Middle Ages. Whereas in aristocratic ages there had existed an acknowledged and enforced hierarchy, from the lowest to the highest member of the community, democracy of necessity destroys this system of subordination. Moreover, it cuts every man off also from his ancestors and descendants (beyond one or two degrees), as well as from his contemporaries, for it is the *individual*, and not the family or professional, religious or other corporate bodies, which is regarded as the ultimate self-directing social unit. This process "threatens in the end to confine [the individual] entirely within the solitude of his own heart."[60] As he no longer identifies himself with larger groups and no longer senses the ties of obligation which used to lead him to devote himself to ends and interests beyond himself, he retires into his immediate circle. So dangerous are the results of this "private selfishness which is the rust of society,"[61] that Tocqueville states that his "chief object in writing" *Democracy in America* has been in combating them.[62]

There are a number of ways in which the individualism and hunger for material goods characteristic of the present time conduce to the rise of despotism.

First, if it is true that it is in the nature of the central government to desire always to enlarge its own power, then it must be true that a posture of constant wariness is the only appropriate one for the citizen. But

---

[58] Léo Moulin, "On the Evolution of the Meaning of the Word 'Individualism,'" *International Social Science Bulletin* 6 (1955), pp. 181–185.

[59] *Democracy in America*, vol. 2, p. 104.

[60] Ibid., vol. 2, pp. 104–106.

[61] Ibid., vol. 1, p. 295.

[62] Ibid., vol. 2, p. 310.

individualism militates against this, by drawing men from the participation in public life into their own private concerns. To the extent that this occurs, despotism sees the places of power vacated and steps in.

Furthermore, in situations of actual *coup d'état* from above or revolution from below, the habits of apathy produced by individualism will permit one or the other anti-liberal party to gain control. Thus, Tocqueville concludes, "the proper object ... of our most strenuous resistance is far less either anarchy or despotism than that apathy which may almost indifferently beget one or the other."[63] Otherwise, the complacent selfishness of the people is easily exploited by authoritarian and Revolutionary *condottieri*, who are still quite interested in wielding power.

Of particular importance in the modern period is another factor which would manifest itself increasingly. While conservatives might suppose that love of material enjoyments would lead the masses to become demanding and turbulent, the real danger is that they would instead come to fear the slightest breath of change as a harbinger of disorder and revolution. This point had already been noted by Constant; within the framework of Tocqueville's thought, it can be looked on as the complement of the trend, already mentioned in *Democracy*, for property ownership to become more widespread, and thus for the masses to become more and more attached to the established order. If from one point of view this argued the eventual end of the era of revolutions, and thus the possibility of a permanent liberal order free of the peril of Communist-inspired uprisings from below, on the other hand, it tied the interests of growing numbers of people to the preservation of the *status quo*, regardless of its liberal or illiberal character: "If the slightest rumor of public commotion intrudes into the petty pleasures of private life, they are roused and alarmed by it. The fear of anarchy perpetually haunts them, and they are always ready to fling away their freedom at the first disturbance."[64]

These words are prophetic, for Tocqueville was to see this occurring practically under his own eyes in France, especially after June 1848. It was, indeed, a chief cause of the coming to power of Napoleon III. In 1853, in despair Tocqueville complained to Gobineau that every grocer now "keeps repeating that the people should be kept within bounds to impede the

---

[63]Ibid., vol. 2, p. 388.

[64]Ibid., vol. 2, pp. 149–150, also p. 277.

abolition of Property and Family, and to prevent them from ransacking his grocery ... it is enough for an idea to seem dangerous and a sort of universal silence is drawn around it."[65] In their blind cupidity, it was quite possible that the *bourgeoisie* of France would repeat the experience of their forebearers of the Old Régime, who had been eager to have the protection of the state against the people, and of whom Tocqueville concludes, "No one seemed to have the faintest inkling that the protector might one day become the master."[66]

To some extent, however, the desire for material well-being produces certain correctives for its own deficiencies, Tocqueville maintained. What these are, and the degree to which he had confidence in them, we will investigate later on. Enough has been said, in any case, to indicate the direction from which Tocqueville expected problems to come, both for the human qualities he valued so highly and for the free society he loved.

Summing up, Tocqueville outlined the aims of policy in a democratic age as he saw them:

> To lay down extensive but distinct and settled limits to the action of the government; to confer certain rights on private persons and to secure them the undisputed enjoyment of those rights; to enable individual man to maintain whatever power he still possesses; to raise him by the side of society at large, and uphold him in that position; these appear to me the main objects of legislation in the ages upon which we are now entering.[67]

He had ascertained that among the Americans the causes that tended to maintain the republic fell into three categories.[68] First, there was the "peculiar and accidental situation in which Providence has placed" them. But this was obviously a factor of little relevance to a general theory. Second was "the law." Tocqueville accordingly proposed, as had Constant (and, indeed, many other liberals), a comprehensive system of guarantees against the excessive extension of state power: it included encouragement of private association, secondary public bodies, freedom of the press, independence of the judiciary, and, in general, a respect for political forms.[69]

[65] *European Revolution*, pp. 224–225.
[66] *Old Régime*, p. 69.
[67] *Democracy in America*, vol. 2, p. 347.
[68] Ibid., vol. 1, p. 298.
[69] Ibid., vol. 2, pp. 340–344.

Of the most interest to us, however, is the third factor in the edifice of American freedom, "the manners and customs of the people." It is among these that religious belief as a guardian of freedom is to be found.

That Tocqueville attributed very high priority to reuniting the religious and liberal attitudes, which had been, he thought, artificially and perniciously set at odds by the eighteenth-century writers, has often been noted. In 1836, in explaining the basic idea of *Democracy* (the first volume of which had just appeared), he wrote his friend, Eugène Stoffels, as follows:

> You seem to me to have understood the general ideas on which my programme rests. What most and always amazes me about my country, more especially these last few years, is to see ranged on the one side men who value morality, religion and order, and upon the other those who love liberty and the equality of men before the law.

Rather than being thus aligned against each other, in the true order of things they are united: "It seems to me, therefore," he continues, "that one of the finest enterprises of our time would be to demonstrate that these things are not incompatible; that, on the contrary, they are bound together in such a fashion that each of them is weakened by separation from the rest. Such is my basic idea."[70] It is *à propos* of this conception that Tocqueville, in the same letter, qualifies himself as a "liberal of a new kind."[71]

Tocqueville repeats the same idea in the introduction to the first volume of *Democracy*, and the great importance of religious belief for liberty is underscored throughout both volumes of this work. But there are some more general observations respecting the role of religion in his thinking which ought to be made first, since they have to do not distinctively with the liberal social order, but with any sort of society.

Much as did Constant, Tocqueville proclaims that religious faith is an inherent principle of human nature. Man's existential situation—the

[70] J.-P. Mayer, *Prophet of the Mass Age: A Study of Alexis de Tocqueville* (London: Methuen, 1939), pp. 24–25.

[71] It will be seen that this is not literally true; that, on the contrary, Tocqueville's thought in this area bears a great resemblance to that of Constant. But Tocqueville here was contrasting himself, not really with liberals such as Constant, but "with the majority of democrats of our day."

shortness of his life and the disparity between his heart's desires and the merely partial fulfillment they can obtain from reality—constantly draws his mind to thoughts of a future state, out of which religion grows. "Religion," he concludes, "is simply another form of hope, and it is no less natural to the human heart than hope itself." Thus periods of unbelief (and presumably individual cases of it, as well) are to be explained by unusual circumstances:

> Men cannot abandon their religious faith without a kind of aberration of intellect and a sort of violent distortion of their true nature; they are invincibly brought back to more pious sentiments. Unbelief is an accident, and faith is the only permanent state of mankind.[72]

The glib liberal-progressivist view of the eighteenth-century *philosophes* (and of others), that religion, supposedly founded in ignorance and fear, would continue to retreat before the victorious forces of liberalism and science, was an illusion. Ignorance is by no means necessarily connected with religious faith, Tocqueville asserts, as is demonstrated by the fact that irreligion and a level of culture practically that of savagery coexist in certain parts of Europe, while, on the other hand, "in America, one of the freest and most enlightened nations in the world, the people fulfill with fervor all the outward duties of religion."[73] American civilization, which Tocqueville describes as the product of the spirit of religion and of liberty,[74] is thus a standing negation of the shallow philosophy of history which identifies the march of progress and enlightenment with the decline of religious faith. If any society may be said to presage the future, it is the American, and there religion was thriving.[75]

Despite his confident assertions of the inevitability of religious belief, however, Tocqueville often speaks in such a way as to suggest that he had

---

[72] *Democracy in America*, vol. 1, p. 321.

[73] Ibid., vol. 1, p. 319.

[74] Ibid., p. 45.

[75] Indeed, Tocqueville at times goes even further, maintaining that the crucial role of religion in American society proves something positive about religion in general: "There can be no greater proof of its utility and of its conformity to human nature than that its influence is powerfully felt over the most enlightened and free nation of the earth." Ibid., vol. 1, p. 314.

some anxiety as to the security of faith in the modern world.[76] Thus, in the introduction to *Democracy*, he lists as one of the "first duties" of modern statesmen, "to educate democracy, to reawaken, if possible, its religious faith."[77] If religious belief and particularly the belief in individual immortality are as inherent in human nature as Tocqueville insists they are, it is curious that he expresses himself at a number of points as troubled by the possibility of their fading away. Furthermore, in discussing the French Revolution, he shows that traditional religious sentiments can be replaced by political ones, at least for many people. Thus, what is really involved in his statement that men "are invariably brought back to more pious sentiments" is unclear. Nevertheless, his formal position is one very much like Constant's: there is "implanted" in man "the taste for what is infinite and the love of what is immoral . . . their steadfast foundation is fixed in human nature. . . . [Man] may cross and distort them; destroy them he cannot."[78]

Not only, however, is religious sentiment inevitably a part of human life, but Tocqueville goes on to assert that it is *good* that this is so; and it is good in the first place from the traditional point of view that—contrary to philosophers such as Bayle—a society of atheists is impossible. "Liberty cannot be established without morality," he states, "*nor morality without faith*."[79] In his letters to Gobineau, Tocqueville at one point admits that a certain amount of intolerance must accompany any positive religious faith. He adds, however:

> Yet I am convinced that the eventual damage to human morality thereby caused is far less than what would result from moral systems that have emancipated themselves from religion altogether. The longer I live the less I think that the peoples of the world can ever separate themselves from a positive religion; and this growing conviction makes me less concerned with these inconveniences that are eventually inherent in every religion, including the best.[80]

---

[76]Tocqueville proceeds in this way on a number of issues: he states as certain facts that elsewhere he demonstrates much less than total assurance about. Marvin Zetterbaum notes this and explains Tocqueville's grand proclamations on questions of which he was really of two minds as attempts at self-fulfilling prophecies. "His first consideration," he adds, "is always the effect his thought will have on society." *Tocqueville and the Problem of Democracy* (Stanford, Cal.: Stanford University, 1967), pp. 16–20.

[77]*Democracy in America*, vol. 1, p. 7.

[78]Ibid., vol. 2, p. 142.

[79]Ibid., vol. 1, p. 12. (Italics added.)

[80]*European Revolution*, p. 206.

Like many another thinker who has taken this position, Tocqueville uses the alleged universality of religious belief as an argument for its necessity: "Laws, and especially religious laws, are thus so necessary that there has never been a people of any importance that could do without them."[81]

In his analysis of the religious sentiment which is inherent in man, Tocqueville emphasized the role of the desire for immortality. This was, in fact, central to his view of what a religion is. In warning of the dangers of religious alliances with the state, he contrasts such a foundation for religious strength with the preferable situation, "when a religion founds its empire only upon the desire of immortality that lives in every human heart."[82] In his chapter (in the second volume of *Democracy*) on "How Religious Belief Sometimes Turns the Thoughts of Americans to Immaterial Pleasures," he is almost exclusively concerned with the idea of immortality, and he bluntly (and oddly) states, "Most religions are only general, simple and practical means of teaching men the doctrine of the immortality of the soul."[83] For Tocqueville, therefore, the idea of immortality was what he had most in mind when speaking of religious belief. Given his preoccupation with the ways in which religion conditions and directs human conduct, this was entirely to be expected.

What role, then, does he ascribe to the doctrine of immortality in helping preserve society?

In the first place, Tocqueville maintains that the idea of an afterlife, including supernatural rewards and penalties, is indispensable as a sanction for morality beyond those available on earth.[84] In *Democracy*, after discussing the doctrine of rightly-understood self-interest, which he holds to be a tenable basis for morality in the democratic period, Tocqueville indicates its shortcomings: "If [it] had nothing but the present in view, it would be very insufficient, for there are many sacrifices that can find their recompense only in another." While conceding that not all followers of religion do so in order to further their own interests, he asserts that "self-interest is the principal means that religions themselves employ to govern

[81] Ibid., p. 212.

[82] *Democracy in America*, vol. 1, p. 321.

[83] Ibid., vol. 2, p. 152.

[84] Strictly speaking, the infinite prolongation of this afterlife, or "immortality," is never necessary for Tocqueville's arguments—merely that there be some substantial period of survival after death.

men," and he brings up Pascal's wager as grounds for a rational man to restrict his actions within the limits of morality.[85]

But Tocqueville's chief interest in the doctrine of immortality is not as a sanction for morality in the ordinary sense. In a letter to Gobineau, the following curious passage occurs:

> You seem to contest the social function of religions. Here we assume truly antithetical positions. You say that the fear of God does not stop people from murder. Even if this were true—and I doubt whether it is really true—what is the conclusion? Whether secular or religious, the function of law is not to eliminate crime (which is usually the product of deranged instincts and of such violent passions as will not be halted by the mere existence of laws). The efficacy of laws consists in their impact on society, in their regulation of matters of daily life, and in setting the general temper of habits and ideas.[86]

Here Tocqueville foregoes any particular claim that religious sanctions tend to deter men from committing infringements on the rights of others, meanwhile advancing the strange view that secular sanctions do not deter, and that crime is always or usually a result of instinct or passion. In any event, this is a faithful representation of the relative emphasis he places on the different social effects of religious belief, and especially of the doctrine of immortality. Its most important effect in his view has to do not with adding supernatural sanctions to earthly ones, but with creating a particular sort of mentality.

This has two aspects, corresponding to two related dangers to character in the democratic age.

On one hand, there is a problem of "directing human actions to distant objects." In the absence of belief in an afterlife, men will tend to become short-sighted and direct their attention exclusively to the here and now:

> When men have once allowed themselves to think no more of what is to befall them after life, they readily lapse into that complete and brutal indifference to futurity which is but too conformable to some propensities of mankind. As soon as they have lost the habit of placing their chief hopes upon remote events, they naturally seek to gratify without delay their smallest desires; and no sooner do

[85] Ibid., vol. 2, pp. 133–135.

[86] *European Revolution*, pp. 211–212.

> they despair of living forever, than they are disposed to act as if they were to exist for a single day.[87]

What is to be feared is that men will contract the habit of surrendering to each meaningless desire as it arises, and end by accomplishing "nothing great, permanent and calm."[88]

Ignoring the hyperbole of asserting that those who do not believe they will live forever will act as if they would not survive the day,[89] we may note that when Tocqueville emphasizes here the dangers of giving in to immediate desires, he does not speak of the effects of such conduct on the rights of others, but of its undermining the will and the capacity to create something grand and permanent in one's own life. This was the role played by religion in the ages of faith: it led men to discipline themselves, suppressing momentary desires, in order to bring to pass some grand design which their mind's eye had traced to the future. Tocqueville adds, "This explains why religious nations have so often achieved such lasting results."[90]

The second beneficial effect on the personality of the doctrine of immortality is one which pertains more precisely to any doctrine preaching the existence of a "supersensual and immortal principle, united for a time to matter." Even doctrines maintaining that this principle is extinguished by fusion with the Deity, or that it is transferred to animals, or that it does not undergo rewards and punishments, have the sort of edifying result Tocqueville is discussing. This consists in the fact that it counteracts the dominant tendency of democratic ages towards excessive material gratifications.

In pursuing these tastes, enlightened and educated men, he concedes, will use "honest and lawful" means only; so, once more, we are not dealing with violations of the rights of others in the quest for self-gratification. Rather, the danger is "that in the end [man] may lose the use of his sublimest faculties, and … may at length degrade himself. Here and here only, does the peril lie." So great is this peril, that

[87] *Democracy in America*, vol. 2, pp. 158–159.

[88] Ibid.

[89] We may remark in passing that Tocqueville too frequently indulges in such hyperbole, verging on—or passing into—the absurd: e.g., "In Europe, almost all the disturbances of society arise from the irregularities of domestic life … the European endeavors to forget his domestic troubles by agitating society." Ibid., vol. 1, p. 315.

[90] Ibid., vol. 2, p. 158.

> It should therefore be the unceasing object of the legislators of democracies and of all the virtuous and enlightened men who live there to raise the souls of their fellow citizens and keep them lifted up towards heaven.[91]

Materialists and others who preach that there can be no mind separated from the body are to "be marked as the natural foes of the whole people."[92]

In addition to the value attributable to the doctrine of immortality as an encouragement to habits of long-range planning and as a method of diverting men's attention from physical enjoyments to higher pursuits, religious belief fulfills another role, not less important. It provides men with a coherent set of answers to the most important questions in life, and thus affects their minds and characters through this avenue also.

In regard to the manner in which such beliefs should be arrived at, and the spirit in which they ought to be held, Tocqueville freely admits that ideally the way of the rational man, fully aware of the claims of alternative beliefs, is best. He speaks of three distinct states of the human intellect. The first is one in which "a man believes firmly because he adopts a proposition without inquiry." To this succeeds a state of doubt, which finally produces a situation of conviction once more, but now a conviction founded on rational examination. "This time he has not a dim and casual glimpse of the truth, but sees it clearly before him and advances by the light it gives."[93] But Tocqueville qualifies this picture in two ways. In the first place, it is doubtful whether the sort of conviction characteristic of men who have thrown off their self-imposed intellectual minority "arouses as much fervor or enthusiastic devotion in men as does their first dogmatical belief." Furthermore, and most important, it is a path which is reserved for an élite:

> We may rest assured that the majority of mankind will always remain in one of these two states, will either believe they know not wherefore, or will not know what to believe. Few are those who can ever attain to that other state of rational and independent conviction which true knowledge can produce out of the midst of doubt.[94]

---

[91] Ibid., vol. 2, p. 154.

[92] Ibid.

[93] Ibid., vol. 1, p. 196. As we shall see presently, such rational conviction, even in the best of cases, is available to the individual only on a relatively few issues: uncritical faith on most questions must be the rule.

[94] Ibid., vol. 1, pp. 196–197.

And, in fact, in describing the condition of Europe in his own time, he paints it as corresponding to the second of the states described above. In evident anguish, he depicts an age in which all moral norms have undergone ruthless analysis, and none are accepted with any degree of assurance:

> has man always inhabited a world like the present, where all things are not in their proper relationships, where virtue is without genius, and genius without honor . . . where the light thrown by conscience on human actions is dim, and where nothing seems to be any longer forbidden or allowed, honorable or shameful, false or true?[95]

This situation of "intellectual wretchedness" is characteristic of democratic times, Tocqueville believes. The "Cartesianism" rife in such periods acts as a solvent of all received truths, and many will spend a lifetime bereft of any firm conviction. Moreover, there is a constant social mobility in democratic societies, and the influence which social position has in creating opinions cannot act so as to fix them for an individual for any length of time.[96]

Such a condition is likely to be merely transitional, however. Dogmatic belief "may change its object and its form; but under no circumstances will [it] cease to exist, or, in other words, men will never cease to entertain some opinions on trust and without discussion."[97] This is evident from the common argument that, if one attempted philosophically or scientifically to demonstrate for oneself the truth of every proposition on the basis of which one acted, action would be indefinitely postponed (even assuming that all individuals had the ability to undertake such demonstrations). In addition, Tocqueville maintains that in order for a society to exist and prosper, it is necessary that the citizens should share certain general notions on a number of important issues,[98] which is quite improbable if each went about selecting his fundamental ideas for himself. Thus, for both the individual and for society, an acknowledged source of basic life-shaping ideas is required.

It is here that we begin to see the specific value religion should hold for those interested in preserving liberty. In democratic ages, the overwhelming temptation will be to seek the source in the views of the majority

---

[95] Ibid., vol. 1, pp. 13–14.
[96] Ibid., vol. 2, p. 74.
[97] Ibid., vol. 2, pp. 9–12.
[98] Ibid., vol. 2, p. 9.

of people: "Not only is common opinion the only guide which private judgment retains among a democratic people, but among such a people it possesses a power infinitely beyond what it has elsewhere." The long-range danger, then, does not lie in the direction of intellectual chaos (just as, politically, it is not anarchy that is ultimately to be feared), but in a monolithic tyranny of majority opinion; what must be avoided is the pitfall that for traditional religion is substituted pious obedience to public opinion, with the majority acting as the highest spiritual authority.[99] It is *à propos* of this danger that Tocqueville speaks of a new "physiognomy of servitude" that may be waiting to be discovered by democratic man and adds:

> there is here matter for profound reflection of those who look on freedom of thought as a holy thing and who hate not only the despot, but despotism. For myself, when I feel the hand of power lie heavy on my brow, I care but little to know who oppresses me; and I am not the more disposed to pass beneath the yoke because it is held out to me by the arms of a million men.[100]

It is within this framework that we must view Tocqueville's discussion of the value of religion as a means of providing men with "fixed and determinate" ideas on fundamental issues. In a democracy, the individual will find the source of such ideas either in a religious authority or in the majority of his fellow citizens, for the Kantian and liberal notion that the autonomous individual may with the aid of reason legislate for himself in these matters is an illusion.

Indeed, one of the greatest tasks for religion in the democratic age is to condition the majority to legislate for itself certain self-denying ordinances in the moral realm. This is the basic reason why the connection between religion and liberty in the United States, which Tocqueville found taken for granted by the Americans, is so instructive. Although when he is concerned to emphasize the dangers of the tyranny of the majority, he

---

[99] Ibid., vol. 2, p. 12.

[100] Ibid., vol. 2, p. 13. Tocqueville is well aware that what is presented as the will of the majority is often simply the will of a party posing as the majority's spokesman. What occurs is that a certain group of radical revolutionaries claim to represent the people, and then takes this to entail that it possesses the "right of doing whatever it chooses and despising what men have hitherto respected, from the highest moral laws to the vulgar rules of common sense." Ibid., vol. 1, p. 434.

is skeptical of the extent of real freedom in the United States (e.g., his blanket statement: "freedom of opinion does not exist in America"[101]), at most other times he pictures it as a free country and links this freedom with the remarkable religiosity of the people. The fact is, he states, that the majority respects certain restrictions on its power: on the one hand, the established individual rights guaranteed by law and, on the other, the principles of "humanity, justice and reason."[102] Respect for Christian morality and equity sets up barriers to the heedless trampling on individual rights. It is ultimately because of these influences, he holds, that "no one in the United States has dared to advance the maxim that everything is permissible for the interests of society, an impious adage which seems to have been invented in an age of freedom to shelter all future tyrants."[103]

The benefits for society, and particularly for democratic society, accruing from religious faith are nowhere treated more extensively by Tocqueville than in the chapter in the second volume of *Democracy* entitled (somewhat misleadingly, for its scope is much greater), "How Religion in the United States Avails Itself of Democratic Tendencies." In this chapter he sums up and elaborates on a number of his chief notions on the subject, and it thus appears useful to consider the course of his argument in some detail.

Tocqueville begins by positing an extremely idealistic view of human behavior:

> There is hardly any human action, however particular it may be, that does not originate in some very general idea men have conceived of the Deity, of his relation to mankind, of the nature of their own souls, and of their duties to their fellow creatures. Nor can anything prevent these ideas from being the common spring from which all the rest emanates.[104]

It would perhaps be best to modify this to assert that hardly any human action is *unconditioned* by such beliefs. So fundamental and pervasive are these ideas that "doubt on these first principles would abandon all their actions to chance and would condemn them in some way to disorder and impotence."

[101] Ibid., vol. 1, p. 275.
[102] Ibid., vol. 1, p. 434.
[103] Ibid., vol. 1, p. 316.
[104] Ibid., vol. 2, p. 21.

At this point Tocqueville makes a decisive break with at least the implied position of liberals who have not seen religion as playing so crucial a role in the life of society: he denies the possibility or practicality of a rational solution to these questions. Tocqueville was all his life singularly unimpressed by the discipline of philosophy. To Gobineau, for instance, he remarks: "It is typical of philosophical debates that neither of the participants emerges dissuaded from his original opinions. Thus it is best not to dispute; it saves effort."[105] In regard to the question immediately at issue, he observes, in the chapter we are discussing:

> philosophers are themselves almost always surrounded with uncertainties ... in spite of all their efforts, they have discovered as yet only a few conflicting notions, on which the mind of man has been tossed about for thousands of years without ever firmly grasping the truth or finding novelty even in its errors.[106]

Since all available evidence indicates that it is not possible to arrive at settled notions concerning these issues through the use of critical reason, and since Tocqueville is convinced of their overwhelming importance for human affairs, he concludes that at this juncture religion must enter: "The first object and one of the principal advantages of religion is to furnish to each of these fundamental questions a solution that is at once clear, precise, intelligible and lasting, to the mass of mankind."[107] As he observes elsewhere, "What is most important to meet among men is not any given ordering, but order."[108]

So far Tocqueville has discussed the value of religion from the viewpoint, not of a liberal society, but of insuring qualities of mind conducive, as he himself states, to the "happiness and greatness" of mankind in this world. This was clearly implied in his calling on religion to supply the means of preventing all human action from being condemned "to disorder and impotence." Now, however, he goes on to state that what he has asserted is "especially true of men living in free countries." For, in the absence of religion, we have the intellectual chaos described above: "doubt gets hold of the higher powers of the intellect and half paralyzes all the

---

[105] *European Revolution*, pp. 210–211.
[106] *Democracy in America*, vol. 2, pp. 21–22.
[107] Ibid., vol. 2, p. 22.
[108] Ibid., vol. 2, p. 194.

others. Every man accustoms himself to having only confused and changing notions on the subjects most interesting to his fellow creatures and himself." Tocqueville concludes that this situation will result, in the first place, in a cowardly refusal to continue thinking about the humanly most important issues: "in despair of ever solving by himself the hard problems respecting the destiny of man, he ignobly submits to think no more about them."[109] Such a situation of moral confusion will have a tendency to lead to despotism, for the individual now finds himself burdened with an "excess" of freedom. He is called upon to decide too many things for himself, and, since certainty must constantly elude him, he is required to decide these all simultaneously and, as it were, continually:

> When there is no longer any principle of authority in religion any more than in politics, men are speedily frightened at the aspect of this unbounded independence. The constant agitation of all surrounding things alarms and exhausts them. As everything is at sea in the sphere of the mind, they determine at least that the mechanism of society shall be firm and fixed; and as they cannot assume their ancient belief, they assume a master.[110]

From this he deduces, "I am inclined to think that if faith be wanting in [man], he must be subject; and if he be free, he must believe."[111]

Tocqueville already made a similar point in regard to the United States, where, he maintained, political freedom and independence of thought are only possible by virtue of a restriction of independence in moral and religious questions:

> In the moral world everything is classified, systematized, foreseen and decided beforehand; in the political world everything is agitated, disputed, and uncertain.... These two tendencies, apparently so discrepant, are far from conflicting; they advance together and support each other.[112]

[109]This is surely a strange direction for Tocqueville's argument to take: the whole point of the argument for religious faith which he is considering here is that certain key issues must be withdrawn from individual judgment and be accepted blindly. It is unclear why declining to think about these questions because one does not believe answers are possible is more ignoble than making the sacrifice of the intellect and refusing "to lift the veil of the sanctuary" of such questions.

[110]*Democracy in America*, vol. 2, pp. 22–23.

[111]Ibid., vol. 2, p. 23.

[112]Ibid., vol. 1, pp. 142–143. At other times, however, Tocqueville is at pains to

A related argument is given by Tocqueville at another point in *Democracy*. So far he has maintained that the fixity of views in the moral and religious areas is beneficial to the preservation of free governments because it removes possible sources of anxiety that might lead people to demand such fixity in the political area through despotism. He adds now that such determinateness is valuable also because it sets limits to the tendency of the human mind in a democratic situation to innovate in politics:

> the human mind is never left to wander over a boundless field; and whatever way may be its pretensions, it is checked from time to time by barriers that it cannot surmount. Before it can innovate, certain primary principles are laid down, and the boldest conceptions are subjected to certain forms which retard and stop their completion.... These habits of restraint recur in political society and are singularly favorable to the tranquility of the people and the durability of the institutions they have established.[113]

A last argument along these lines is that, in the absence of certainty concerning the higher things, men are thrown back on the pursuit of their material interests, since these appear to them now as the only settled and tangible reference points in a chaotic world.[114]

The desirable state of affairs, where stable institutions furnish a backdrop to the calm and productive lives of the citizens, is to be contrasted with what obtained in France during the great Revolution. There all religious and political institution were simultaneously called into question and remodeled. As a consequence, total confusion prevailed, and all customary limits were removed. Out of this moral swamp there emerged a new and very sinister species of being: "Revolutionaries of the hitherto unknown breed came on the scene: men who carried audacity to the point of sheer insanity; who balked at no innovation and, unchecked by any scruples, acted with an unprecedented ruthlessness."[115] Tocqueville thus interprets

emphasize the fundamental *stability* of political principles in the United States, beneath all the apparent upheaval of ideas: "the general principles of government are more stable and the chief opinions which regulate society are more durable [in the United States] than in many other countries.... The same tendency of opinion has been observed in England, where for the last century greater freedom of thought and more invincible prejudices have existed in any other country in Europe." Ibid., vol. 1, pp. 195–196.

[113]Ibid., vol. 1, pp. 315–316.

[114]Ibid., vol. 1, p. 197.

[115]*Old Régime*, p. 157.

the Terror and the other excesses of the Revolution, not simply as a series of responses to such events as foreign invasion of France, the collapse of the currency, etc., but as a product of a deeper moral transformation in the people and, particularly, the leaders.[116] The latter, whom Tocqueville characterizes as "strange beings," did not pass away with the Revolution, however. Rather, that Revolution which first created them as it proceeds in its course, continues to bring them forth: "a new race of men who subsequently made good and proliferated in all parts of the civilized world, everywhere retaining the same characteristics. They were already here when we were born, and they are still with us."[117]

Tocqueville's analysis of the real character of the French Revolution and of the revolutionary movements which have continued it into his own day provides another, less obvious, argument for the necessity of religious belief and ought to be noticed at this point. For Tocqueville interpreted the Revolution as much more a religious than a political phenomenon in the traditional sense. The universality and comprehensiveness of its principles, its methods of propaganda, the fervor it aroused in its disciples, and its grand aim—to create a New Man by regenerating society—all stamp it as "a species of religion."[118] Significantly, Tocqueville connects the birth of this new religion with the eclipse of the old one: "When religion was expelled from their souls [i.e., the French], the effect was not to create a vacuum or a state of apathy; it was promptly, if but momentarily, replaced by a host of new loyalties and secular ideals."[119] As with religion at its purest, so too this new religion was able to rouse men to feats of heroism and self-sacrifice. In these few remarks, Tocqueville adumbrates what was to become a familiar religionist interpretation of the twentieth-century God that failed: the vision and fervor of totalitarian movements

[116] Ibid., p. 205.

[117] Ibid., p. 157. During 1848, Tocqueville had come into contact with some of this "new race": Blanqui, who "seemed to have passed his life in a sewer" and the very "recollection of whom has always filled me with horror and disgust"; and Barbès, "one of those men in whom the demagogue, the madman, and the knight-errant are so closely intermingled ... and who can only make their way in a society as sick and troubled as ours. I am inclined to believe that it was the madman that predominated in him." Alexis de Tocqueville, *Recollections*, trans. by Alexander Teixeira de Mattos (New York: Meridian, 1959), pp. 130–131.

[118] *Old Régime*, pp. 10–13.

[119] Ibid., p. 156.

derive, it is alleged, from a warped and rechanneled religious impulse. Totalitarianism only becomes possible when the process of secularization of life has advanced to a high degree.

Most important among religion's contributions to freedom, however, is the circumstance that all religion to one degree or another, but especially Christianity, implant in men a motivation which acts as a partial antidote at least to typically democratic attitudes. Tocqueville here raises once more the question of "individualism" (in the sense previously discussed), which "tends to isolate [men] from one another, to concentrate every man's attention upon himself; and ... lays open the soul to inordinate love of material gratification. The greatest advantage of religion is to inspire diametrically contrary principles."[120] Because democratic people tend to be more pleasure loving than others, the value of religion as a means of raising men to a higher ground is greater among such nations.

❧

It is clear from what has gone before that Tocqueville conceived of religion as offering a *possible* extra-rational and authoritative solution for some of the problems of democratic society. What is difficult to judge is whether he thought it *necessary* that such a solution should be resorted to as a substitute for rational persuasion.

The problem occurs primarily because of a chapter in the second volume of *Democracy*, "How the Americans Combat Individualism by the Principle of Self-Interest Rightly Understood." Here he outlines how the more elevated and self-sacrificing ethical systems of aristocratic times have been replaced, in that laboratory of the democratic experience that is the United States, by another doctrine "that man serves himself in serving his fellow creatures and that his private interest is to do good." This is an example of a modern people having become aware of the inevitability of a certain degree at least of "individualism" and having come to terms with it by turning it to advantage. The Americans

> have found out that in their country and their age, man is brought home to himself by an irresistible force; and, losing all hope of stopping that force, they turn all their thoughts to the direction of it. They therefore do not deny that every man may follow his own

[120] *Democracy in America*, vol. 2, p. 23.

> interest, but they endeavor to prove that it is the interest of every man to be virtuous.[121]

The linking up of personal hedonism in this way with social utilitarianism is another manifestation of the increasing "rationality" of the world. In words that might have been written by any number of social thinkers from Burke to Max Weber, Tocqueville asks:

> Do you not see that religious belief is shaken and the divine notion of right is declining, that morality is debased and the notion of moral right is therefore fading away? Argument is substituted for faith, and calculation for the impulse of sentiment.[122]

But, with the sort of resigned realism that contributed to distinguishing him from more conservative observers of the same process, he asserts that one must accept this new state of affairs as given and take advantage of some of its own features to mitigate its worst potentialities:

> If, in the midst of this general disruption, you do not succeed in connecting the notion of right with that of private interest, which is the only immutable point in the human heart, what means will you have of governing the world except fear?[123]

Tocqueville concedes that this new ethical system is more likely to produce moderation and regularity than any spectacular acts of self-sacrifice. Nevertheless, it will serve its function if, while not generating many acts of saintly virtue, it induces the great majority of mankind to comply with the minimal demands of morality. He therefore gives it his endorsement:

> I am not afraid to say that the principle of self-interest rightly understood appears to me the best suited of all philosophical theories to the wants of men of our time, and that I regard it as their chief remaining security against themselves. Towards it, therefore, the minds of the moralists of our age should turn; even should they judge it to be incomplete, it must nevertheless be adopted as necessary.[124]

[121] Ibid., vol. 2, pp. 129–130.
[122] Ibid., vol. 1, p. 255.
[123] Ibid.
[124] Ibid., vol. 2, p. 131.

This endorsement is consistent with Tocqueville's policy of acquiescing in those shortcomings of democracy which appear to be inevitable, and attempting to remedy them as much as possible. In the present case, we see emerging a rational, individualistic system of ethics, and a program of education is called for: "Educate, then, at any rate, for the age of implicit self-sacrifice and instinctive virtues is already flitting far away from us, and the time is fast approaching when freedom, public peace, and social order itself will not be able to exist without education."[125]

In the United States, where education is widespread, the doctrine of rightly understood self-interest is effective, Tocqueville maintains; the average American "obeys society ... because he acknowledges the utility of an association with his fellow men and he knows that no such association can exist without a regulating force."[126] Similarly, with another area the temporary sacrifice of the individual's interest for his own long-range greater interest is sometimes required; that of property. Here, too, Tocqueville asserts that the modern ethic adequately fulfills its purpose: "The lower orders in the United States understand the influence exercised by the general prosperity upon their own welfare."[127] In America, "the doctrine of interest rightly understood ... is as often asserted by the poor man as by the rich."

The Americans have arrived at the final term of a process of the rationalization of the civic spirit. Tocqueville describes a sequence of three stages in the history of the individual's association of his own fate with that of his nation. These stages correspond to those which he analyzed in the case of belief (which was to be expected, since these basic human attitudes are all undergoing the same transformation). It will be remembered that the progress was from "instinctive" belief to doubt and confusion and then on to rational belief. Similarly with the feeling of patriotism, there is a primitive sort of patriotic feeling which is founded on faith, comparable to a religion; there is, in addition, however, a more "rational" sort, based on the individual's perception of the connection between his personal well-being and that of his country. In this case, patriotism becomes the product of egoism, resulting as it does from the benefits which the individual draws from his country and from his identification of himself with it.

---

[125] Ibid., vol. 2, p. 132.
[126] Ibid., vol. 1, p. 67.
[127] Ibid., vol. 1, p. 253.

Between these two stages, there may occur a situation much like that which Tocqueville so often ascribes to contemporary Europe, when the first sort of patriotism is dying or dead, and the second has not yet been fully accepted. Again, his realism leads him to side with the inevitable: "In this predicament to retreat is impossible, for a people cannot recover the sentiments of their youth any more than a man can return to the innocent tastes of childhood. . . . They must go forward."[128]

Although all this is clear enough from a number of important passages in Tocqueville's works, nevertheless it is difficult to assess its significance, since he often writes in a contrary sense. At times, that is, he assumes that the individual must derive the great bulk of the rules of social morality not in a rational manner from a consideration of his own long-range self-interest, but rather in an "authoritarian" manner as imposed from above. He advises sincere liberals, for instance, who are personally anti-religious, to desist from attacking religious opinions, for "despotism may govern without faith, but liberty cannot":

> How is it possible that society should escape destruction if the moral tie is not strengthened in proportion as the political tie is relaxed? And what can be done with a people who are their own masters if they are not submissive to the Deity?[129]

At other times, moreover, he directly implies the inadequacy of enlightened self-interest by stressing the impulsiveness and shortsightedness of democratic nations. Thus, he declares that "the people are more apt to feel than to reason," which makes sustained sacrifice, such as is often required in wartime, difficult for democracies.[130] This general tendency is easily observable in the United States, he asserts:

> The difficulty that a democracy finds in conquering the passions and subduing the desires of the moment with a view to the future is observable in the United States in the most trivial things. The people, surrounded by flatterers, find great difficulty in surmounting their inclinations; whenever they are required to undergo privation or any inconvenience, *even to attain an end sanctioned by their own rational conviction*, they almost always refuse at first to comply.[131]

[128] Ibid., vol. 1, pp. 250–252.
[129] Ibid., vol. 1, p. 318.
[130] Ibid., vol. 1, p. 237.
[131] Ibid., vol. 1, p. 238. (Italics added.)

In discussing the dangers threatening property in situations of universal suffrage (where the masses are propertyless), he states that there will be a certain amount of legalized spoliation. At this point he unmistakably assaults the doctrine of rightly understood self-interest:

> In vain will it be objected that the true interest of the people is to spare the fortunes of the rich, since they must suffer in the long run from the general impoverishment which will ensue. Is it not the true interest of kings, also, to render their subjects happy, and of nobles to admit recruits into their order on suitable grounds? If remote advantages had power to prevail over the passions and exigencies of the moment, no such thing as a tyrannical sovereign or an exclusive aristocracy could ever exist.[132]

The same sort of disenchantment with rational self-interest as a sufficient guarantee of moral action is shown in another passage, strikingly contradictory to ones quoted above:

> The inhabitants of the United States talk much of their attachment to their country; but I confess that I do not rely upon that calculating patriotism which is founded upon interest and which a change in the interests may destroy.[133]

He adds that "A government retains its sway over a great number of citizens far less by the voluntary and rational consent of the multitude than by that instinctive, and to a certain extent involuntary, agreement which results from similarity of feelings and resemblances of opinion."[134]

How are we to reconcile these contradictory statements? On the one hand, Tocqueville maintains that the coming age will depend for the sense of political obligation, for devotion to country and to one's fellow man, on voluntary and rational consent, based on the perception that one's self-interest will be promoted by such a course. He asserts further that such a course is viable, given "education" in the new "American" morality.

On the other hand, he appears to hold that the masses are scarcely capable of far-sighted action, of letting the present good go for the sake of the greater future reward, and adds at one point an attack on the sort of

[132]Ibid., vol. 1, p. 222.
[133]Ibid., vol. 1, p. 409.
[134]Ibid.

calculating patriotism he has said is the inevitable (and acceptable) form that that feeling will take in the future!

It is obvious from this that Tocqueville himself had not decided the question of whether rational self-interest was a sufficient basis on which to build the ethical code of the coming democratic society. Sometimes, his patrician disdain for the limited moral resources of the masses of men overcomes his hopes for the future, and one can glimpse the fervent wish that things were not the way they are.

Indeed, there is evidence that Tocqueville came to doubt the view expressed in *Democracy* that rational self-interest as the basis is even compatible with—let alone complementary to—a fundamentally religious attitude, as shown by the fact that the two were joined inextricably in the ethos of the Americans. In discussing with Gobineau the character of various moral systems, he sharply *contrasts* those oriented towards the afterlife with those founded on self-interest:

> When the vision of the next world becomes obscure it is again natural that people who are still unable to live without moral sanctions will try to find them on this earth and that they will thus create all these systems which may be different but which are all concerned with the doctrine of human interest. And when the vision of eventual heavenly rewards is accordingly lost, it is again logical that people should be more and more attached to the only prospects that remain before them, to the benefits of this world.[135]

Tocqueville here links self-interest with the fading away of the religious outlook: "I think that something similar may have happened during the decline of paganism, and that it is typical of the decline of all religions. The mass comes forth and reveals its instincts, and it will find philosophers who will make doctrines to fit them."[136] In fact, throughout the correspondence with Gobineau, which concerns itself at times with the question of religion and morality, Tocqueville displays a position much more "traditional" than in *Democracy*, and the viability of self-interest as the basis of morality in the future is not maintained.

At last, in *The Old Régime and the French Revolution*, Tocqueville, apparently having forgotten his earlier views altogether, states unequivocally,

---

[135] *European Revolution*, pp. 206–207.
[136] Ibid.

"Nor do I think that a genuine love of freedom is ever quickened by the prospect of material rewards." Often, in point of fact, it is despotism that can provide—at least as a short-term matter—superior lures in this respect. What really attaches men to liberty is, simply, its intrinsic value, and genuine love of liberty is something that, Tocqueville confesses, "defies analysis."[137]

The measure of Tocqueville's lack of faith in the efficacy of enlightened self-interest is in part his emphasis on the indispensability of religious belief in democracy. This emphasis receives added significance when we consider Tocqueville's own religious views.

There is really no need to enter into the controversy revolving around Tocqueville's Catholic faith or lack of it. While believing scholars have been at pains to depict him as one of theirs (one of them going so far as to indulge in a bit of pious fraud), the evidence seems conclusive on the other side. He never speaks in his candid moments of confession of faith, of any beliefs peculiarly Catholic, or even Christian; and to Gobineau he stated flatly, "Je ne suis pas croyant (ce que je suis loin de dire pour me vanter), mais tout incroyant que je sois."[138] It is difficult to see why such a remark would be made by anyone who was "philosophically speaking ... a Catholic with an aristocratic, Jansenist, Pascalian bent."[139]

The more interesting question is, given that Tocqueville did not himself believe in Christianity, what then is the status of his injunctions to "moralists" and others, to do their utmost to preserve Christian belief.[140] Is it the case that, as a number of more recent critics have charged, Tocqueville is proposing the employment of "social myths," which he knows to be false, but which he strongly believes also to be necessary for the preservation of the sort of society he valued? One writer speaks of Tocqueville's

[137] *Old Régime*, pp. 168–169.

[138] Alexis de Tocqueville, *Œuvres Complètes*, ed. by J.-P. Mayer (Paris: Gallimard, 1959), vol. 9, p. 57.

[139] John Lukacs, "Comment on Tocqueville Article," *French Historical Studies* 2, no. 1 (Spring, 1961), p. 123, n.

[140] Although he generally speaks in favor of the preservation of religious belief, for the Western world it is Christianity which is at issue, since Tocqueville reiterates the impossibility of founding a new religion in the present circumstances of society.

"acceptance of a deliberately manipulated myth designed to enforce or sustain a particular pattern of moral response";[141] another applies this analysis to other issues as well, concluding that, for Tocqueville, "Free society stands or falls by a specific obfuscation against which political philosophy necessarily revolts."[142]

There is no doubt that many remarks of Tocqueville's would seem to confirm this interpretation. Thus, he states:

> If it be of the highest importance to man, as an individual, that his religion should be true, it is not so to society. Society has no future life to hope for or to fear; and provided the citizens profess a religion, the peculiar tenets of that religion are of little importance to its interests.[143]

This same attitude is implied in the fact that when Tocqueville himself discusses the bases of morality, he does not have recourse to a religious explanation, but limits himself to naturalistic terms. Thus, in distinguishing between the true moral code and the codes of "honor," which vary according to class, nation and epoch, he states:

> Mankind is subject to general and permanent wants that have created moral laws, to the neglect of which men have ever and in all places attached the notion of censure and shame: to infringe them was *to do ill*; *to do well* was to conform to them.[144]

And in maintaining the existence of a standard of justice over and above the demands of a political majority, he asserts:

> I hold it to be an impious and detestable maxim that, politically speaking, the people have a right to do anything.... A general law, which bears the name of justice, has been made and sanctioned, not only by a majority of this or that people, but by a majority of mankind.... When I refuse to obey an unjust law, I do not contest the right of the majority to command, but I simply appeal from the sovereignty of the people to the sovereignty of mankind.[145]

---

[141] Lively, op. cit., p. 197.

[142] Zetterbaum, op. cit., p. 160. The words are quoted from Leo Strauss.

[143] *Democracy in America*, vol. 1, p. 314.

[144] Ibid., vol. 2, p. 242. (Italics in original.)

[145] Ibid., vol. 1, p. 269.

Although this argument for salvaging majoritarianism is perhaps a bit too ingenious, it nevertheless indicates Tocqueville's personal reluctance to resort to a religious foundation for his ethical beliefs.

Again, the correspondence with Gobineau, where Tocqueville, as we have seen, admits his lack of faith and yet insists in the strongest terms on the indispensability of faith for social purposes, would seem to point in this direction. Moreover, the same point arises in a different context in these letters, for, in later years, their disagreements centered not on the social usefulness of religion, but on Gobineau's racial theories. Here, too, Tocqueville emphasized the social effects of these ideas. He was particularly concerned, since he felt that, as a deterministic theory, it would tend to aggravate certain pernicious modern trends:

> What I disapprove of in the book I told you before: it is less the work itself than its tendency, which I consider dangerous. If we were to suffer from excessive enthusiasm and self-confidence, as did our ancestors of 1789, I would consider your book a salutary *cold shower*. But we have disgracefully come to the opposite extreme. We have no regard for anything, beginning with ourselves; we have no faith in anything, including ourselves.[146]

And he quite clearly disclaims the point of view that a theory of this kind is to be judged solely on its scientific merits: "by studying German I have not yet become enough of a German to be captivated so much by the novelty or by the philosophical merits of an idea as to overlook its moral or political defects."[147] To this sort of attitude, Gobineau responded curtly: "My book is research, exposition, presentation of facts. These exist or they don't. There is nothing else to say."[148]

But it appears to me that to speak of Tocqueville's championship of "social myths" is to state the case too strongly; a somewhat different perspective, more compatible with the facts would, I think, eliminate whatever element of sinister mythmaking, suggestive of the Platonic "noble lie," that might at first seem to lurk in Tocqueville's position.

In the first place, the views which Tocqueville is castigating for their deleterious social consequences are not ones whose truth has been demonstrated. We have already noticed his judgment on the inconclusiveness

[146] *European Revolution*, p. 270. (Italics in original.)
[147] Ibid., p. 232.
[148] Ibid., pp. 285–286.

of philosophical debates on the "big questions." In regard to racism, Tocqueville in a letter takes up Gobineau's own comparison of his theory to a doctor announcing to his patient that he is mortally ill. Tocqueville states:

> You ask: What is immoral in that? My answer is that even though this act in itself may not be immoral, its consequences assuredly are most immoral and pernicious.... I must add that physicians, like philosophers, are often greatly mistaken in their prognostications; I have seen more than one person condemned by physicians who nevertheless became quite well subsequently and who angrily criticized the doctor for having uselessly frightened and discouraged them.[149]

It seems possible to make out an argument for Tocqueville's position along the following lines: We are dealing with issues on which reason has not decided, but which are of the utmost importance for man in society. Now, certain principles are conducive to human happiness, and indeed, to the very existence of human life, while some are not. Historically, these moral principles have been embedded in evolving systems of symbols. This is probably necessary for the majority of mankind, which cannot be expected to grasp the indispensable ethical principles except as symbolized within the framework of a religion. As Tocqueville puts it, "I firmly believe in the necessity of forms which fix the human mind in the contemplation of abstract truths, and aid it in embracing them warmly and holding them with firmness."[150] An analogy with chess is perhaps possible here. Someone might raise the objection to the game as it is customarily played that the use of *material* appurtenances somehow falsifies the game of chess, which in reality is one of purely ideal relationships, and could be played without actual pieces and board. But he would be missing the point of their use. The case with religion is similar. There is no question of demonstrating the truth or falsity of basic religious doctrines, such as the immortality of the soul, the existence of God, etc. Since these ideas are in fact conducive to a truly human life, they may be referred to as practical "truths." It would be just as foolish to cavil at these truths being presented through the use of particular historically developed systems of symbols, as it would be for someone to object that bishops or rooks in chess ought not to look

[149] Ibid., pp. 291–292.

[150] *Democracy in America*, vol. 2, p. 21.

the way they do, since nothing in the ideal system of the game warrants them looking one way or another. Such an objection would represent a misunderstanding, since the purpose of the pieces is purely instrumental, and the *particular* form they assume is largely a historical "accident." The same may be said of the particular concrete notions of the various religious, e.g., the stories concerning the life of Christ or the ritual of the Mass.

But even conceding that Tocqueville's position on religion in a free society was by no means as Machiavellian as is sometimes suggested, there still remain a number of problems with his conception, problems of which, I believe, he became more conscious in his later years.

The most important of these has to do with the real possibility of religious belief independently exerting a significant effect on the course of social development.

Tocqueville's conception of what brings about changes in society is not the most refined and polished imaginable; nevertheless, it is clear that he believes in some sense that *social*, rather than *economic* or *technological*, factors are of greatest importance. His best known statement on this question is:

> Social condition is commonly the result of circumstances, sometimes of laws, oftener still of these two causes united; but when once established, it may justly be considered as itself the source of almost all the laws, the usages, and the ideas which regulate the conduct of nations: whatever it does not produce, it modifies.[151]

At another point, he states:

> I do not doubt that the social and political constitution of a people predisposes them to adopt certain doctrines and tastes, which afterwards flourish without difficulty among them; while the same causes divert them from certain other opinions and propensities, without any voluntary effort and, as it were, without any distinct consciousness on their part.[152]

---

[151] Ibid., vol. 1, p. 48.
[152] Ibid., vol. 2, p. 153.

It happens that Tocqueville provides a very good example of this process in outlining at one point the development of Christian belief: "it cannot be denied that Christianity itself has felt, to some extent, the influence that social and political conditions exercise on religious opinions."[153] The existence of equality of conditions within society led man to "readily conceive the idea of the one God, governing every man by the same laws ... while on the contrary in a state of society where men are broken up into very unequal ranks, they are apt to devise as many deities as there are nations, castes, classes or families."

The fact that Christianity appeared in the world in the midst of the Roman Empire, where a certain uniformity of law existed, and where each citizen, *vis-à-vis* the Emperor, was so weak as to produce a state of near equality, "necessarily predisposed" men to accept it. With the break up of the Empire and the emergence of feudalism, religion again took on the coloring of the surrounding society. It is not that the general conceptions associated with Christianity were forgotten, but the worship of saints and angels almost brought it down to the level of the superstition-ridden polytheism which it had replaced. As for the future, Tocqueville asserts:

> It seems evident that the more the barriers are removed which separate one nation from another and one citizen from another, the stronger is the bent on the human mind, as if by its own impulse, towards the idea of a single and all-powerful Being, dispensing equal laws in the same manner to every man.[154]

As with Christianity, so with skepticism and doubt: the movements by which the principle of authority in thought has been progressively dismantled in modern history—the Reformation, the scientific philosophy of Bacon and Descartes, the Enlightenment—are traced by Tocqueville to an ever-increasing equality of conditions in society. "Who does not perceive that Luther, Descartes, and Voltaire employed the same method, and that they differed only in the greater or less use which they professed should be made of it?" What, then, determined to what degree the method was employed in each of these cases? Why, for instance, did Descartes permit personal judgment in philosophical questions and not in political ones?

[153] Ibid., vol. 2, pp. 25–26.
[154] Ibid., vol. 2, p. 26.

Why did the eighteenth-century writers extend his method to the latter issues? What determined these facts was the condition of society and the predispositions which this set up in the minds of the public: philosophical doubt "could be generally followed only in ages when [social] conditions had at length become nearly equal and men nearly alike."[155] In a similar way, Tocqueville held that the future democratic age would be particularly threatened by pantheism, the religious view most suitable to it.[156]

He thus saw religious belief and unbelief as, to a large extent, socially conditioned; and this not peripherally, in regard to particular ideas and emphases, but fundamentally. This state of affairs would, of course, continue into democratic times, and he advised religious leaders to become aware of this fact, and take certain measures in view of it, e.g., religious forms must be kept to a minimum. Most importantly, however, religion must be careful not to irritate the masses gratuitously, by condemning the ends which they will inevitably pursue. The reason Tocqueville gives for this is interesting: "For as public opinion grows to be more and more the first and most irresistible of existing powers, the religious principle has no external support strong enough to enable it long to resist its attacks." In America, the clergy are well aware of this situation, and they have accommodated themselves to it. Besides strictly abstaining from involvement in politics, they

> know and respect the intellectual supremacy exercised by the majority; they never sustain any but necessary conflicts with it, . . . they readily adopt the general opinions of their country and their age, and they allow themselves to be borne away without opposition in the current of feeling and opinion by which everything around them is carried along.[157]

The problem that this view raises is clear. If religious belief is so vulnerable to influence from society, and, in particular, from majority opinion (in democratic countries), how will it be able to fulfill its functions as a counterweight to the tendencies of society and of the majority? Tocqueville provides a possible resolution to this problem:

---

[155]Ibid., vol. 2, pp. 5–6.

[156]Ibid., vol. 2, p. 33. Constant, too, considered pantheism a dangerous and destructive force; see *De la religion*, vol. 3, pp. 27–29.

[157]*Democracy in America*, vol. 2, pp. 27–29.

> [T]he principal opinions which constitute a creed, and which theologians call articles of faith, must be very carefully distinguished from the accessories connected with them. Religions are obliged to hold fast to the former, whatever be the peculiar spirit of the age; but they should take good care not to bind themselves in the same manner to the latter.[158]

The example of religion's coming to terms with society which Tocqueville develops at greatest length is that concerning material well-being. This, as we have seen, is one of the prime characteristics of democratic society, and any religion which attempted to suppress this urge would itself be destroyed by it. Rather, "the chief concern of religion is to purify, to regulate, and to restrain the excessive" taste for enjoyments: "men cannot be cured of the love of riches, but they may be persuaded to enrich themselves by none but honest means."[159]

But this does not really solve the problem, for the question arises: Is contempt of riches, for instance, the sort of merely "accessory" opinion, the jettisoning of which is necessary in democratic times, but does not injure the core of Christian beliefs? Tocqueville states that the Americans, "having admitted the principal doctrines of the Christian religion without inquiry, are obliged to accept in a like manner a great number of moral truths, originating in it and connected with it."[160] But when the American clergy seem to see the chief object of a virtuous life, not as a means of heavenly reward, but to happiness on earth[161] are they not violating some important principle of Christian belief? It would seem that love of riches and greater care for success in this world than for the Kingdom of God *are* violations of fundamental Christian notions, brought about by the democratic state of society, and that even where the doctrines of Christianity are accepted, the "moral truths connected with it" are by no means immune to modification by social forces. But in that case, what Christian principles, important for the goal of compensating for democratic defects, are not susceptible to alteration at the hands of democratic society?

Religion is open to conditioning from society in another way, which also would appear to compel qualification of the great hopes Tocqueville,

[158] Ibid., vol. 2, p. 27.
[159] Ibid.
[160] Ibid., vol. 2, p. 7.
[161] Ibid., vol. 2, pp. 134–135.

in *Democracy*, places in religious belief for a free society. Religious faith, as the example of France since the eighteenth century shows, can be decisively class conditioned.[162]

It has on occasion been noticed, though not, I think, sufficiently appreciated, how closely Tocqueville's thought at times comes to that of Karl Marx. Particularly is this true in regard to his notion of the inception and expansion of ideas in society; although he has nothing like a comprehensive theory of "ideology," he often assumes that the perception of social class interest is crucial for the explanation of the spread of a particular idea at a particular time. This is quite to be expected in a thinker who held that "social condition" is "the source of almost all the laws, usages, and ideas which regulate the conduct of nations."[163] Time and again, Tocqueville traces the assent of an idea to the social position of the individuals involved. This occurs especially in his account of the vicissitudes of religious belief in France since the eighteenth century, and it creates another dilemma for his general theory of the role of religion in a liberal society.

On a number of occasions—in his conversations with Nassau Senior, in his *Souvenirs* and in *The Old Régime*—Tocqueville examines the problem of how the Voltairean nobility of the *ancien régime* and the anticlerical liberal *bourgeoisie* of the Restoration and the July Monarchy had, by the mid-nineteenth century, turned once more to the Catholic faith. Discussing the almost personal hatred of religion manifested by some of the *philosophes*, he asks, "What Frenchman of today would dream of writing books like those of Diderot and Helvétius, and, supposing anyone were to do so, who would read them?" The reason for this altered state of affairs is, he thinks, to be found in the new use for religious faith discovered in the last sixty or seventy years by those who have come to fear for the stability of all social institutions, particularly property:

[162]Earlier, in the first volume of *Democracy in America*, Tocqueville had traced the "unnatural" prominence of irreligion in France to the "close connection of politics and religion. The unbelievers of Europe attack the Christians as their political opponents rather than as their religious adversaries" and propose a divorce of religion and politics. Ibid., vol. 1, p. 325. But, as he was to see later on (discussed below), it was not religion's connection with politics per se, but rather its alliance with anti-liberal, anti-*bourgeois* forces, that caused its unpopularity with the middle classes. Later, the latter were to welcome religious support for their own claims.

[163]Ibid., vol. 1, p. 48.

> Trained in the hard school of successive revolutions, all the various classes of the French nation have gradually regained that feeling of respect for religious faith which once seemed lost forever. The old nobility, which before 1789 had been the most irreligious class, became after 1793 the most pious; first to be infected with disbelief, it was also the first to be "converted." Once the *bourgeoisie* woke to the fact that its seeming triumph was likely to prove fatal to it, it, too, developed leanings towards religion. Thus little by little religion regained its hold on all who had anything to lose in a social upheaval and unbelief died out, or anyhow hid its head the more these men became alive to the perils of revolution.[164]

It is true that the above—which is reproduced in similar terms in the other places mentioned—is not a completely "Marxist" interpretation of the issue: it seems to account, for instance, for the aristocracy's tendency towards unbelief in the eighteenth century, not by its class interest, but by intellectual "fashion." Nevertheless, he relies on class interest to explain the change.

But this interpretation entails certain difficulties for Tocqueville. In his conversations with Senior, he remarked that it took the Revolution of 1848 to reconvert the middle classes: "They too see the want of the religious sanction; they now wish to join the aristocracy in imposing its restraints on the people. None but the lowest classes now profess irreligion."[165] But if the middle classes have come around to Christianity in response to the threat of the lower classes, as the nobility had in response to that of the *bourgeoisie*, on what basis are we to expect the lower classes to renew their religious faith? Tocqueville's view that belief is the natural state of man, and unbelief an accident, is not helpful here; if that were truly the case, then it would have been employed to explain the conversion of the upper classes, and yet Tocqueville did not do so. Thus, on his class analysis of the causes of belief and unbelief, there is no reason to look for the conversion to religion of that class from which many of the pressures on the liberal social order may be expected to come.

How the newly found, opportunistic faith of the middle classes might be expected to effect the conversion of the lower classes is indicated by Tocqueville. Senior paraphrases his remarks as follows:

---

[164] *Old Régime*, pp. 154–155.

[165] *Correspondence and Conversations*, vol. 1, pp. 106–107.

> That the instinct which leads the mass of mankind to assume the existence and the influence of a supernatural Being is so strong that it will always prevail unless it is violently opposed. That a religious system which is taught in every school, preached from every pulpit, and treated by all the educated portion of society as if it were true, will be received without examination by nine-tenths of those to whom it is offered and adopted and retained by them without suspicion[*sic*].[166]

But this is surely placing the prospects for a religious revival among the lower classes in too favorable a light. It assumes something like a monopoly of control of the means of communication of opinion, such as religious forces enjoyed in the United States, and which Tocqueville seems to have approved of there.[167] If it required actual threat to their chief values and way of life for the middle classes to be weaned away from Voltaireanism, why should mere propaganda from *bourgeois* sources be sufficient to accomplish the same thing for the working classes, particularly considering that Tocqueville foresees a great advance in educational opportunities for them, and, since, moreover, there is in existence an influential class of socialist publicists who will not conveniently oblige the middle classes in their campaign?

Finally, the dependence of religious belief on the general state of society also affects Tocqueville's claim that it will provide an antidote for "individualism." For, not only will religion itself undergo the same modifications and influences which have brought this kind of feeling to the fore in society at large, but Tocqueville seems clearly to be overestimating the effect that

[166]Ibid., p. 107.

[167]"Freedom of opinion does not exist in America. The Inquisition has never been able to prevent a vast number of anti-religious books from circulating in Spain. The empire of the majority succeeds much better in the United States, since it actually removes any wish to publish them.... In the United States no one is punished for [licentious] books, but no one is induced to write them.... In this case the use of power is good." *Democracy in America*, vol. 1, p. 275. The question is whether Tocqueville qualifies as "good" the suppression only of "licentious" books, or of anti-religious ones as well. In any case, this break with civil libertarianism would not be unique in his thought. Already at the beginning of *Democracy*, he quoted approvingly John Winthrop's "fine definition of liberty," which distinguished sharply between "liberty [for a man] to do what he lists ... a liberty to evil as well as to good ... that wild beast, which all the ordinances of God are bent against"; and, on the other hand, "a liberty to that only which is good, just and honest ... the same kind of liberty wherewith Christ hath made us free." Ibid., vol. 1, pp. 44–45.

preaching and exhortation can have on social developments. We ought to recall how the older society forestalled the evil in question. In earlier times, the social system was so structured that almost everyone felt his fate bound up with that of a number of others: members of guilds and other professional associations; those in the feudal hierarchy with other nobles, and particularly with those above and below them in the system; citizens of the same city, enjoying special privileges which had to be conquered from authority and fought for even afterwards; aristocrats and their retainers; even lords and peasants. Individualism came into existence with the breakdown of this system.[168] It is the scheme of values, the "code of honor," corresponding to democratic times, as sacrifice for the interest of the group corresponds to aristocratic times. Since the actual life conditions of people are constantly pushing them in the direction of withdrawal from social affairs, it seems far-fetched to suppose that mere preaching by religious authorities and the acceptance of certain theological doctrines by the people can make a real difference in this trend.

It is, of course, open to Tocqueville to insist that even if religion cannot make a *great* difference in stemming the tide of materialism and individualism, it can make *some* difference, and thus it is important for moralists and others to increase its authority wherever possible. But then this sort of subdued claim hardly justifies the assertion that the resurrection of religious belief is one of the greatest tasks of our age, nor supports the significance Tocqueville ascribed to his own work of reconciling liberalism and religious faith.

By the last years of his life, Tocqueville seems to have largely despaired of religion's playing a key role in the preservation of freedom. For one

[168] "That word 'individualism,' which we have coined for our own requirements, was unknown to our ancestors, for the good reason that in their days every individual necessarily belonged to a group and no one could regard himself as an isolated unit." *Old Régime*, p. 96. He observes, too, of the middle classes in France, before the Revolution: "The utmost concern was shown for [the interests] of the group. For the members were acutely aware that they had to defend their group privileges and prestige; no individual could play for safety and make ignoble concessions, hoping to pass unnoticed. The stage on which each played his part was small but brightly lit, and there was always the same audience to applaud or hiss him." Ibid., p. 115.

thing, he observed with disgust the support given by the Catholic Church to the Second Empire. He remarks of the French in 1856:

> we now have become extremely devout. Everyday the pastor of our village upholds from the pulpit the Christian virtues of the Emperor, his faith, his charity and the rest ... At this time when we are more exclusively than ever preoccupied with the material goods of this earth we advance every day along this road of sanctimoniousness.[169]

Particularly in the foreword to *The Old Régime* (1856) does this same disillusionment with religion appear. Here he expresses many of the old fears for the future of liberty; the great problem is still "individualism," which is encouraged by the despot, since it plays so well into his hands. But now Tocqueville maintains that it is only participation in public affairs that can protect against tyranny. The individual practice of a Christian life is perfectly compatible with the existence of an unfree society; saintly Christians did, after all, live under the worst of the Roman Emperors. And that this was possible should not be difficult to understand, for "the patrimony of the Christian faith is not of this world."[170] It is not unlikely that Tocqueville, the lifelong student of Rousseau, was well aware of how this notion echoes that in the *Contrat social* (in the chapter on "La religion civile"): "Le christianisme est une religion toute spirituelle, occupée uniquement des choses du ciel ; la patrie du chrétien n'est pas de ce monde."[171]

Instead, what Tocqueville attaches his hopes to is "freedom," in the sense of the right to take part in public affairs. It alone is capable of elevating men above "mere mammon worship and the petty personal worries which crop up in the course of everyday life, and of making them aware at every moment that they belong each and all to a vaster entity above and

[169] *European Revolution*, p. 293. This last sentence indicates that Tocqueville has either changed his mind on the notion in *Democracy* of the compatibility of great concern for material gratification and religious faith, or that he never really took that notion seriously.

[170] *Old Régime*, p. xiv. At about the same time, in his notes for the continuation of this work, Tocqueville makes an allied point when he attacks moralists, "surtout parmi les chrétiens," for ignoring the duties one has towards one's country and one's fellow citizens, and emphasizing only those towards humanity and one's neighbor. The real value of patriotic feeling in promoting moral development has been completely neglected he complains. *Œuvres complètes*, vol. 2, pp. 346–347.

[171] Rousseau, bk. 4, chap. 8.

around them—their native land."[172] In this way, Tocqueville appears to be edging towards an awareness of the dilemma presented by the Christian faith for anyone who attempts to stir men to heights of civic mindedness and a sense of responsibility to the commonwealth, a dilemma which Rousseau saw plainly. For, ultimately, Tocqueville's thought is oriented more towards a re-establishment of community than towards making viable the new moral world of "atomistic" individualism. As one writer recently put it:

> From Plato and Aristotle, through Burke and De Tocqueville, the therapeutic implication of social theory is remarkably consistent: an individual can exercise his gifts and powers fully only by participation in the common life. This is the classical ideal. The healthy man is in fact the good citizen. The therapeutic and the moral were thus connected in the Western tradition of social theory.[173]

But, as Tocqueville had long understood, Christianity lacked any great interest in patriotism or the civic virtues: these pertained rather to antiquity, and had been *replaced* by Christianity.[174] Unlike the ancient republics, Christianity sets up a moral order superior to that of the state, and teaches that *there* is every man's true homeland. In this way, the same element in the Christian worldview which liberals such as Laboulaye and Acton saw as the beginning of individual freedom—the institution of an ideal realm of moral obligation to whose claims those of the state were strictly subordinated—in the end proved to be at odds with Tocqueville's demand for a rebirth of the civic spirit.

---

[172] *Old Régime*, p. xiv.

[173] Philip Rieff, *The Triumph of the Therapeutic* (New York: Harper and Row, 1966), p. 68.

[174] *European Revolution*, p. 192.

CHAPTER 3

Lord Acton

In attempting to clarify Acton's position on the interconnection of religion and freedom, it must be kept in mind that a consistent attitude cannot be gleaned from his works as they now stand, since on crucial points they contain a number of contradictions. The explanation of this is to be sought in the long-run evolution which took place in Acton's thinking, amounting in the end to a change of such an extent as to require a reclassification of him in the spectrum of political thought: the writer who began as an orthodox, if genial, Burkian, ended as a radical liberal of a rather unique sort.

The two greatest formative influences on Acton were the fact of his having been born into a Roman Catholic family with close connections to the great Catholic aristocracies of the Continent; and his inherited association, through his stepfather and others, with the Whig aristocracy of Britain.[1] As a young man and burgeoning scholar, particularly under the direction of Döllinger, Acton quickly emerged as a conservative Whig, excited by the renaissance of Catholic scholarship, especially in south Germany, and eager to demonstrate what he believed to be intimate relationship between the principles of English Constitution and the Roman Catholic Church.

[1] Gertrude Himmelfarb, *Lord Acton* (Chicago: University of Chicago, 1962), pp. 4–9.

In the view of the early Acton, there existed a "Catholic notion of the State,"[2] which, when properly investigated, would turn out to have at its root principles analogous to those which activated the English Constitution:

> I think that there is a philosophy of politics to be derived from Catholicism on the one hand and from the principles of our constitution on the other ... I conceive it possible to appeal at once to the example and interest of the Church and to the true notion of the English Constitution.[3]

In this connection he mentions the philosophical truth that "only the true religion corresponds with the truth in politics. Else there is sure to be a break somewhere in the harmony,"[4] indicating, as it were, a metaphysical basis for the correspondence of the systems of ideas which he considered as most closely approximating the truth in religion and politics respectively. Indeed, he felt that English Catholics, as "the only permanently conservative element in the state," were "the heirs of the establishment."[5] As an enemy of modern democracy, of the Revolution of which Tocqueville wrote, Acton in this period could refer with satisfaction to "the two great conservative powers, England and Rome [the papacy]."[6]

Characteristic of the young Acton was an exaggerated admiration for Edmund Burke, whom he thought of at this time as "the law and the prophets" in political philosophy.[7] The fundamental reason for enlisting himself under the banner of Burke may well lie in what Acton conceived to be the Irishman's connecting of the two traditions. As he wrote a correspondent:

> I would try to get up few such essays as the following: Edmund Burke as a teacher for Catholics. In the writings of his last years (1792–1797) whatever was Protestant or partial or revolutionary of 1688 in his political views disappeared, and what remained was a purely Catholic view of political principles and history. I have much to say about this that nobody has ever said.[8]

---

[2]*Lord Acton and His Circle* (Correspondence), ed. by Abbot Gasquet (New York: Franklin, 1968), p. 79.

[3]Ibid., p. 3.

[4]Ibid., p. 228.

[5]Ibid., p. 32.

[6]Ibid., p. 72

[7]Ibid., p. 60.

[8]Ibid., p. 4.

As we shall shortly see, his commitment to the traditionalist Whiggism of Burke tended to dissipate with time, to the point where he could tell Mary Gladstone (although jokingly to be sure): "I would have hanged Mr. Burke on the same gallows as Robespierre."[9]

The shift in Acton's thought is most plainly to be seen in regard to the question of Catholic persecution. His early conservatism had brought him to the verge of the reactionary Catholic position of the earlier part of the century. In 1860 he wrote that while in certain departments the Spanish Inquisition had been an "unmitigated evil," people had generally overlooked "its really great merit," that of having acted as a guardian of the popular morality and having eradicated certain crimes and vices. The man of whom later on, at Cambridge, students were to say that "he had the Inquisition on the brain"[10] in his uncompromising hostility, at this time praised it as an instrument of "humanity, morality and subordination."[11]

In a similar vein, Acton wrote to his co-worker on the *Rambler*, Simpson, in 1861:

> In [Oxenham's] notice of Guizot was a passage which would have made us obnoxious to the Index. To say that persecution is wrong, nakedly seems to me first of all untrue, but at the same time it is in contradiction with the solemn decrees, with Leo X's Bull against Luther, with a Breve of Benedict XIV of 1748, and with one of Pius VI of 1791.[12]

The later Acton, as is well known, reversed the reasoning implicit in this passage, and, beginning with a moral condemnation of religious persecution, went on to condemn the popes and other ecclesiastical authorities who had condoned or championed it. "The Vatican system," he was later to conclude, as a final judgment, "stands or falls with the doctrine that one may murder a Protestant."[13]

Acton's evolution is discernible also in his attitude towards Whiggism. While he was, from first to last, an opponent of Toryism, and saw it as a system of pure expediency and special interests masquerading as a

---

[9] F. E. Lally, *As Lord Acton Says* (Newport, R.I.: Pioneer, 1942), p. 128.

[10] G. E. Fasnacht, *Acton's Political Philosophy* (London: Hollis and Carter, 1952), p. 190.

[11] Lally, op. cit., p. 216.

[12] *Lord Action and His Circle*, p. 243.

[13] Lord Acton, *Letters to Mary Gladstone*, ed. by Herbert Paul (London: Macmillan, 1905) p. 136.

legitimate political party,[14] towards the later part of his life, Whiggism also came to some extent under the cloud of the same accusation.

In 1863, when he was still cherishing the idea of a Catholic system of politics, and trying to establish its relationship to the principle of the English Constitution, he wrote:

> the essence of Whiggism is the acknowledgment of the supremacy of the divine will, or as we should say, if the term had not been degraded, of divine right, over the will of man, whether represented by the sovereign or by the people, in the institutions of the past, or in speculative theories.... It upholds the laws of the country; but it clings to their spirit, not the temporary forms by which the spirit is expressed or secured. In this way Selden shared in the Great Rebellion, Somers justified the Revolution, and Burke defended the constitutional idea in the American and the revolutionary wars.[15]

Later, however, he reproached Whiggism with a relative lack of commitment to principle, and distinguished it from liberalism, contrasting it unfavorably with the latter. He confessed to "identifying [liberalism] altogether with morality,"[16] and to Lady Blennerhassett he wrote:

> Les Whigs aussi voulaient la liberté, et ils voulaient l'obtenir, s'il le fallait, par la Révolution, c'est-à-dire, au prix du bien-être social. Mais ils y voyaient bien plus un privilège qu'un droit, et plutôt un droit qu'un devoir. Ils la demandaient pour eux plus que pour les autres, selon les conditions locales, les traditions nationales.... Le Libéralisme, chose moderne, est sorti du XVIIIe siècle, et des mains des hommes qui repoussaient les conditions de la vie anglaise, que les Whigs acceptaient en s'y adaptant.[17]

Acton's gradually changing judgment on the great English Whig tradition can best be understood as part of the evolution of his views on the whole subject of the historical idea, of the emphasis on the slow growth and development of institutions, which was the great contribution to social science of certain late eighteenth-century British and, especially, Scottish thinkers, and of the Romantic movement. Acton's early position is one of orthodox Burkeanism. In discussing the constitutional history of England

[14]Ibid., p. 158.

[15]Quoted in Lally, op. cit., pp. 216–217.

[16]Lord Acton, *Selections from the Correspondence of the First Lord Acton*, ed. by J. N. Figgis and R.V. Laurence (London: Longmans, 1917), p. 54.

[17]Ibid., p. 278.

and the development of the historical liberties of the English people, for example, Acton wrote, in 1863:

> Every appeal against oppression was to hereditary rights; the only protection which Englishmen knew was in the traditional laws of the country. By means of this perpetual recurrence to old principles, and of the gradual contrivance of new forms in which to secure their action, the English people conquered their freedom.... When this was neglected, and scope was given to a new faith, or new ideas derived from foreign examples, the result was the establishment of tyranny.... The one thing that saved England from the fate of other countries was ... the consistent, uninventive, stupid fidelity to that political system which originally belonged to all the nations that traversed the ordeal of feudalism.[18]

By the time he delivered his two lectures on the history of freedom, Acton had revised his view of the supreme role of tradition in this area: the achievement of religious freedom in England is ascribed not to fidelity to received ways, but to a deliberate rejection of them. At the beginning of the constitutional struggles of the seventeenth century,

> The only accepted appeal was to tradition. Patriots were in the habit of saying that they took their stand upon the ancient ways, and would not have the laws of England changed ... [however] the oracle of precedent sometimes gave responses adverse to the popular cause. In the sovereign question of religion, this was decisive, for the practice of the sixteenth century, as well as of the fifteenth century, testified in favor of intolerance.... But an age of stronger conviction had arrived; and men resolved to abandon the ancient ways that led to the scaffold and the rack, and to make the wisdom of their ancestors and the statutes of the land bow before an unwritten law.[19]

Acton never entirely abandoned the orthodox Whig interpretation of how the liberties of England had come to be; but with time a relative shift of emphasis emerged in his thought, a putting of the idea of slow growth and evolution towards liberty in its proper perspective, and an appreciation of the value of the "existential" element of a here and now witness and commitment on the part of men to the abstract moral law of liberty. This is particularly evident in his interpretation of the American Revolution.

---

[18]Quoted in Lally, op. cit., p. 54.

[19]Lord Acton, *Essays on Freedom and Power*, ed. by Gertrude Himmelfarb (New York: Meridian, 1956), p. 103.

It was apparently impossible for the later Acton to overestimate the importance for the history of liberty of the American Revolution.[20] The Revolution had rescued freedom in the world:

> Aucun dogme de plus sûr en politique que celui-ci : La liberté allait mourir en Europe à partir de 1773, et c'est l'Amérique qui lui a donné la vie. C'est des forêts, non pas de la Germanie mais de la Pennsylvanie, qu'elle nous vient, telle que nous la voyons.[21]

To Acton the legal claims of the Americans were highly dubious, if not altogether invalid. At one time he wrote to Lady Blennerhassett:

> il n'est nullement prouvé que l'Angleterre ait eu tort légalement. Je ne décide pas ; mais je constate que les premiers jurisconsultes, Blackstone et Mansfield, ne le croyaient pas, que Burke doutait, que Macaulay même ne doute pas du tout de notre droit.[22]

On another occasion he is more definite, and writes: "Si, en politique, le droit dépendait de la loi, leurs adversaires anglais avaient raison."[23] The great merit of the Americans, in fact, consisted precisely in their adherence to the moral code of freedom, independent of any legal or constitutional basis whatsoever:

> Le problème posé par les Américains était, au fond, celui-ci : Doit-on risquer l'existence de son pays, de sa famille, donner sa fortune à la ruine et ses enfants à la mort, verser le sang à flots, renoncer à tout ce qui est établi par l'autorité et sanctifié par la coutume, pour une idée qui n'est écrite nulle part, qui est du pur idéal, qui est spéculative et nouvelle, en contradiction avec la constitution, avec les lois de son pays et des autres, qui n'a pour elle ni sanction religieuse, ni crédit légal, qui est inconnue à tous les codes et à tous les législateurs ? La réponse affirmative, c'est la Révolution, ou comme nous disons le Libéralisme.[24]

In this sense, the doctrines of the American Revolution were more profound than those of the Whiggish revolutions of the seventeenth century: "Les doctrines de 1640 et de 1688 avaient moins de portée. On pouvait les adopter sans être libéral dans toute la force du mot."[25]

---

[20] Gertrude Himmelfarb, *Victorian Minds* (New York: Knopf, 1968), pp. 189–193.

[21] *Acton's Correspondence*, p. 277.

[22] Ibid., pp. 295–296.

[23] Ibid., p. 278.

[24] Ibid.

[25] Ibid., p. 280.

The greatest significance of Acton's giving priority to the American as against the English revolutions is that it indicates a decisive turning away from the Whiggish-Catholic complex of ideas which had determined his early thought, to a more doctrinaire, individualistic and abstractly moral point of view. As late as 1878 Acton had written in a Whiggish vein of "the true law of the formation of free States ... [which may be expressed] by saying that constitutions are not made, but grow."[26] And yet, when Bryce, ten years later, gave expression to essentially the same views, in connection with the founding of the American Republic,[27] Acton composed a review in which he greeted them with scorn: "I descry a bewildered Whig emerging from the third volume with a reverend appreciation of ancestral wisdom, Burke's *Reflections*, and the eighteen canons of Dort, and a growing belief in the function of ghosts to make laws for the quick." Acton's own mature opinion is one of moderation, avoiding both excessive rationalism and what he regarded as an all-too-fashionable exaggeration of the historical idea. As he wrote to a correspondent:

> Bryce ... pense que les choses se font par le ministère du temps, que la vie vient des racines naturelles, que la tradition règne, que rien ne dure, au soleil, qui ne soit préparé par un travail souterrain. C'est ainsi que parlaient Leibniz, Burke, Savigny, le Professeur [Döllinger], tous ceux qui appliquent à la vie universelle les doctrines particulières au droit romain, au droit anglais, à L'Église Catholique, au Positivisme, à l'évolutionnisme. Je crois que cela est faux, comme loi de l'histoire, et je n'ai voulu dire que cela ; c'est-à-dire soulever un doute sur l'historicisme de mon ami. Je ne nie pas, bien entendu, l'immense part de vérité et de force dans ce principe : je voudrais faire la part du principe contraire, qui, en temps et lieu, dans certaines conditions, et sous des points de vue importants, aurait son droit ou aurait eu sa force.[28]

---

[26] *Freedom and Power*, p. 110.

[27] E.g., "The spirit of 1787 was an English spirit, and therefore a conservative spirit.... The American constitution is no exception to the rule that everything which has power to win the obedience and respect of men must have its roots deep in the past, and that the more slowly every institution has grown, so much the more enduring it is likely to prove.... There is a hearty Puritanism in the view of human nature which pervades the instrument of 1787.... No men were less revolutionary in spirit than the heroes of the American Revolution."

[28] *Acton's Correspondence*, p. 296.

The question remains, however: what led Acton to separate himself from the English Whig tradition and from the system he had fashioned for himself?

The fact of the matter is that Acton's earlier championship of what may be called historicism, as he had gathered it from Burke, from early nineteenth-century German thought, and from other sources, was decisively tempered by his growing realization of the tension between this and the idea of an eternal and universal moral law. As Constant had once put it, while under the spell of historicism, "tout est bon, tout est mauvais, selon les lieux."[29] But the ethical relativity implicit in the view of all institutions and systems of ideas as adaptations to the social circumstances of a particular period, which writers like Constant and Tocqueville could at times accept, was proving increasingly distasteful to Acton's moral sense. He was unable to admit of any progress or development in the moral code. The antagonism between the two views was made agonizingly clear to Acton by the inability of his old master Döllinger (whom he customarily referred to as "the Professor") to accept or even fully understand Acton's own concept of the historian as judge; it was on the basis of historicist premises that Döllinger pleaded extenuating circumstances for those past statesmen whom Acton regarded as merely wholesale criminals. More and more Acton came to see the moral law as virtually an independent entity, transcending history and all institutions, including the Catholic Church. It thus became possible to suppose that at certain times and under certain favorable conditions, men acting in history would come to the same insight, act accordingly, and in this way accomplish a "historical leap," which could not be fully accounted for by the historicist approach.[30]

---

[29] *Œuvres*, p. 262.

[30] E. L. Woodward, "The Place of Lord Acton in the Liberal Movement of the Nineteenth Century," *Politica* 4 (1939), p. 260. Cf., Hugh A. MacDougall, *The Acton-Newman Relations* (New York: Fordham University Press, 1962), p. 141, who states: "By 1879 Acton had developed into an inflexible judge who deemed it the duty of the historian to decide on the moral guilt or innocence of historical characters. The historian could make no allowance for time or place. If he tried to mitigate the guilt of those who had committed crime in the past, he was as worthy of reprobation as the criminal he sought to excuse."

Acton's position on the relationship of freedom and religion can best be studied by dividing the subject into two parts: first, the philosophical and analytical, having to do with the conceptual and theoretical interrelationship of morality, religion and freedom; and, second, the historical, concerning the role which religion—and, in particular, Christianity—has played in the evolution of freedom over roughly the past 2,800 years. As will be indicated, there are, of course, points at which the two areas overlap; nevertheless, they can be separated for purposes of analysis.

Regarding the first, analytical and philosophical part, an understanding would be facilitated by identifying Acton's answers to a number of key questions:

1. What is the relationship between freedom and morality?

2. What is the relationship between morality and religion? Specifically, is religious faith either a necessary or a sufficient condition for an effective moral code?

3. What is the relationship between Christianity, and Catholicism in particular, and morality?

The relationship between freedom and morality was for Acton a very close, not to say intimate, one. Thus one is inevitably struck by the idealistic cast of his thought when he deals with the subject of freedom. Freedom for him was not a good of the same kind as other goods, such as wealth, scientific progress or happiness; it was incommensurable with these, and an increment of liberty could not, therefore, be weighed against an increment of some other desirable thing. Nor is liberty to be valued as the means to some other good. As more than one commentator has pointed out, there is no trace in Acton either of the narrower utilitarian argument for freedom—that in some intelligible sense a free society will tend to maximize welfare—or of the wider utilitarianism associated with Humboldt and Mill, that a free society, by multiplying potential centers of innovation, will tend to maximize progress.[31] Welfare, while an increasingly significant value for Acton as he grew older and came to see more truth in the socialist,

[31] Crane Brinton, *English Political Thought in the Nineteenth Century* (London: Hamish Hamilton, 1933), pp. 200–201; see also Woodward, loc. cit., p. 265.

and particularly the *kathedersozialistisch* position,[32] was never an end in itself, but primarily a means to prevent the growingly victorious masses from interfering with the liberal order. And, as he reiterates, a brilliant society of the sort that would presumably be brought about by the unhindered proliferation of new ideas and of experiments in living, was no ultimate end for him. Rather, the justification of a free society lay for Acton in the fact that (a) it was in an important sense *synonymous* with the realization of the moral order, and (b) it provided the individual with the requisite scope for the fulfillment of his moral obligations.

The crucial concept for Acton in this connection is that of *rights*. It is true that, as at least one commentator has noted, Acton had no strong or enduring interest in metaphysics or even philosophy generally, in this way resembling both Constant and Tocqueville; hence, his ideas on this subject tend to be difficult to disentangle. But it is clear that he believed in the existence of a "higher law," "written on the tablets of eternity," from which certain natural rights may be derived.[33] These rights are not socially or governmentally accorded; they are logically and temporally anterior to positive law. They come ultimately "not from civilisation but from nature, by reason of the divine image in the soul."[34]

But while he was an adherent of the doctrine of natural rights, Acton's political philosophy does not begin with the positing of these rights. Rather, the logical sequence commences with the fact of *duty*, and it is from that that the fact of *right*, is derived.

It is generally acknowledged among ethicists that the existence of a right entails that there exists a claim (or claims) on the part of the person possessing the right, which others are morally obliged to respect—A's right to liberty entails that there is a duty on the part of A's fellows not to interfere forcibly with his action, as long as A remains an innocent and peaceful citizen. For most liberals of the natural rights school, it is rights which are primary, with their corresponding duties on the part of others following from them. The special place of Acton in the liberal tradition appears at least partially traceable to the fact that he reverses this order.

Acton was heavily influenced in this line of thought by the nineteenth-century Swiss moralist and Protestant theologian, Alexandre Vinet, for

[32] See for instance, *Letters to Mary Gladstone*, pp. 70, 72.

[33] Quoted in Lally, op. cit., p. 153.

[34] Lionel Kochan, *Acton on History* (London: Deutsch, 1954), p. 70.

whom he had a very great admiration (he listed an exposition of Vinet's thought by Astié among the world's great books).[35] The rationale for the existence of rights which Acton accepted is put more clearly by Vinet:

> Tout devoir emporte un droit : il n'est pas de droit plus sacré que celui de remplir son devoir ; c'est même ici-bas le seul droit absolu ; car le droit s'appuie sur une nécessité primitive ; or le devoir est la première des nécessités, et, à la rigueur, la seule nécessité.[36]

Vinet was the thinker who, in Acton's view, made "Conscience and Liberty a law in Church and State,"[37] and his conception of the supreme importance of conscience is reflected in Acton's perpetual appeal to this tribunal in his discussions of politics and morality. Of conscience, Acton writes: "elle est suprême ; les états et les églises, l'opinion et la tradition, la coutume et le caractère national, les intérêts publics et les droits acquis plient devant elle et ne sont plus que sécondaire."[38] Conscience is *logically* tied to liberty: "The proper name for the rights of conscience is liberty";[39] and "liberty is the reign of conscience."[40] (Actually, this last point might more precisely be put—within Acton's own framework—by saying that liberty is the reign of conscience in the *public* realm; its reign in the private sphere Acton refers to as "virtue.")

In Vinet's exposition, conscience was a primitive faculty of human nature, which renders it a necessity to us "to make our actions harmonize with our convictions.... It is nothing but the sentiment of obligation, in its greatest purity, and most perfect abstraction."[41] His *Outlines of Theology* begins with an exposition of his concept of conscience, and rightly so; for in his view, it "constitutes the identity of the moral man, since deprived of this organ man would be man no longer." Conscience may or may not be enlightened: that is, it may or may not operate in accordance with the moral law. Nevertheless, it is the "foundation [on which] God reconstructs man." As long as conscience is respected, it is possible to rectify false ideas

---

[35] Fasnacht, op. cit., p. 242.
[36] Ibid.
[37] Ibid., p. 146.
[38] *Acton's Correspondence*, p. 279.
[39] Lord Acton, *Lectures on the French Revolution* (New York: Noonday, 1959), p. 227.
[40] MacDougall, op. cit., p. 179.
[41] Alexander Vinet, *Outlines of Theology* (London: Strahan, 1866), pp. 2–3.

of duty and attach man to the true moral code.[42]

Vinet asserts that, seen from an absolute standard, every other good is qualitatively inferior to the pursuit of duty as taught by conscience. Compared to duty, "talent, science, industry, public prosperity, national glory, all are mere child's play."[43] If one were to negate conscience, then the moral being perishes altogether. Thus, Vinet arrives at the indefeasible right of conscience:

> if it so happened that any given law were opposed to that which conscience enforced on us as a duty, we must of necessity obey conscience rather than that law, conscience being above the law, and thus the very moral principle in virtue of which we obey human authority, would irresistibly impel us to resist that authority.[44]

When Acton defines liberty as "the assurance that every man shall be protected in doing what he believes his duty against the influence of authority and majorities, custom and opinion,"[45] it becomes clear that he has accepted Vinet's evaluation of the significance of conscience for man as a moral being, and sees the justification of liberty in the existence of an ideal and absolute set of duties.

This was, we may note, a position which Acton did not substantially alter in the course of his career. As early as 1860, he maintained that it was a fundamental element of the "Catholic notion" of the state, as against the ideas of the modern world: the former defines "liberty not as the power of doing what we like, but the right of being able to do what we ought," and thus provided a firmer foundation for individual freedom.[46]

Acton's manner of presenting his ideas in this area could conceivably lead to misunderstanding, however. The duties which men owe their fellows Acton sometimes chooses to refer to as "the rights of God." Thus, he criticizes John Morley:

> He sees nothing in politics but higher expediency and no large principles. As there are, for him, no rights of God, there are no rights of man—the consequence, on earth, of obligation in Heaven.[47]

---

[42] Ibid., pp. 4–6.

[43] Ibid., p. 10.

[44] Ibid., p. 16.

[45] *Freedom and Power*, p. 55.

[46] Quoted in MacDougall, op. cit., pp. 68–69.

[47] *Letter to Mary Gladstone*, p. 179.

And, on another occasion, he affirms that "the rights of man on earth are the consequence of the rights of God in heaven."[48]

Acton believed that the higher liberal vision was the one he proposed, where rights were not viewed from the vantage point of a possessive individualism, as part of the original "property" of the individual, which he consequently was justified in defending against all would-be aggressors; rather, he emphasized the logical primacy of the bond of interpersonal obligation. He criticized his fellow liberals in a manuscript note: "Liberty and morality. How they try to separate them—to found liberty on rights, on enjoyments, not on duties. Insist on their identity." Liberty, he thought, "is not the realisation of a political ideal: it is the discharge of a moral obligation."[49] Thus, he praises the sects of the seventeenth century for coming upon the great idea of

> sanctifying freedom and consecrating it to God, teaching men to treasure the liberties of others as their own, and to defend them for the love of justice and charity more than as a claim of right [which] has been the soul of what is great and good in the progress of the last two hundred years.[50]

And in praise of the American revolutionaries, he writes:

> le système du droit naturel, des principes abstraits, du droit absolu, *du droit comme forme du devoir*, de la politique entendue comme science et non comme expédient—ce système est entré comme un fer tranchant dans le monde par les jurisconsultes de Boston et les théoriciens de Virginie.[51]

The position of the young Acton on the question of the connection between morality and religion was consonant with his general conservative approach, as has been outlined above. In fact, in 1861, he not only affirmed that morality depended on religion, but went on to adduce this as a justification for religious persecution:

[48] Quoted in Kochan, op. cit., p. 70.

[49] *Letter to Mary Gladstone*, p. 73.

[50] *Freedom and Power*, p. 104.

[51] *Acton's Correspondence*, p. 280. (Italics added.)

> as the preservation of morality depends on the preservation of faith, both alike are in the interest and within the competence of the State. The Church of her own strength is not strong enough to resist the advance of heresy and unbelief. Those enemies find an auxiliary in the breast of every man whose weakness and whose passions repel him from a Church which imposes such onerous duties on her members.[52]

As late as 1878, he reaffirmed his belief that morality was dependent on religious faith. In speaking of the decline of morality in late fifth-century Athens, he stated:

> It was a very short step from the suspicion of Protagoras, that there were no gods, to the assertion of Critias that there is no sanction for laws. If nothing was certain in theology, there was no certainty in ethics and no moral obligation. The will of man, not the will of God, was the rule of life, and every man and body of men had the right to do what they had the means of doing. Tyranny was no wrong, and it was hypocrisy to deny oneself the enjoyment it affords.[53]

As time went on, Acton's conviction in this regard began to dim. To be sure, he never lost a certain apprehensiveness concerning non-religiously based morality: he confided to Gladstone that he could not think the ethical order safe in the hands of the positivists;[54] and to Lady Blennerhassett he communicated the remarkable opinion that utilitarianism was "destitute of any ethical system."[55] Nevertheless, with time he began to part company with the view frequently set forth by Tocqueville of the tight connection of morality and religion, and the moral code, as manifested in conscience, came to have an autonomous validity. Christianity he increasingly saw as "a system of ethics which borrowed its metaphysics elsewhere," rather than "a mere system of metaphysics which borrowed some ethics from elsewhere."[56] It is perhaps not too much to say that a certain deism came to penetrate the thought of Acton in later years; he came to value the "higher morality of a William Penn" more than "the

[52] *The History of Freedom and Other Essays* (London: Macmillan, 1907), pp. 327–328.
[53] Ibid., p. 70.
[54] *Acton's Correspondence*, p. 211.
[55] Quoted in Kochan, op. cit., p. 70.
[56] *Acton's Correspondence*, p. 291.

science of a Bossuet," for instance.[57] In explaining the difference between the Old and the New Whigs (he considered the latter part of the Liberal movement), he attributed it primarily to the idea of conscience cultivated by the sects and coming to flourish towards the end of the seventeenth century. He explains that it could not expand in an atmosphere of reverence for established churches; it only came about

> lorsque le Christianisme s'est trouvé réduit à sa plus simple expression, sans église, sans sacrement, sans clergé, sans rituel, et qu'il est arrivé au point de se confondre avec la morale universelle. Dans cette forme-là le Christianisme a fondé un état.[58]

An indication of what has here been characterized as a sort of incipient deism is contained in a letter of Acton's to Lady Blennerhassett:

> L'Histoire ne peut se servir des systèmes de morale attachés aux religions, car ils ne sont applicables que dans les limites de ces religions. Et une morale indépendante manque à la Science. Il faut donc que l'Histoire se compose son propre système.[59]

Acton goes on to say that history begins by judging according to the criminal codes of all nations, where it finds a few universal principles: no retroactive punishments, the innocent are not to suffer the punishment reserved for the guilty, what is essential for the existence of society must be saved, etc. Now,

> [i]l n'y a d'absolument essentiel que la vie. Donc, c'est la vie humaine qui est l'arche sainte. Personne ne peut être décidément caractérisé et condamné que celui qui verse le sang.... Plus on réussit à étendre cette épreuve, plus l'histoire s'élève au-dessus de l'opinion et entre dans la Science.[60]

This is an interesting passage, and merits some attention. What Acton has done, in his search for an ethical standard to apply in judging actors in history, is, first, to reject the moral system of any religion, because, connected as such moralities are with faith in a theology which sanctions them, they are "inapplicable" to those who do not share the faith. He

[57] Kochan, op. cit., pp. 70–71.
[58] *Acton's Correspondence*, p. 279.
[59] Ibid., p. 281.
[60] Ibid.

turns then to the law, the institutionalized conscience of society, and in a comparison of the laws of all societies he believes he is able to come up with—only a few, it is true—universal principles, assented to by all mankind. The desperate character of Acton's search is revealed by his train of reasoning at this point: it is from the allegedly universal legal principle of "sauver ce qui est essentiel à l'existence de la société," and from the fact that only "life" is essential to society, that he claims to be able to derive the absolute prohibition against shedding blood. The thinness of this reasoning is an indication, it would appear, of the lengths to which Acton was forced to go to find a suitable substitute for a religiously-based moral system. It suggests, too, that he was beginning to move from a religiously-based ethics to one having its foundation in the universal conscience of mankind. The reason for this is not far to seek.

In his earlier period, Acton could accept without devoting too much thought to it the ethical and metaethical beliefs of the ordinary Roman Catholic.[61] Thus, he felt, for example, that the subjectivity of conscience ought to be subordinated to an objective law, which, in the religious domain, was the one transmitted and interpreted by the Church, by virtue of its divine authority. As he became intrigued and then obsessed with the cluster of problems revolving around Ultramontanism, Infallibility and the crimes of the papacy, new and highly disturbing possibilities opened up for him. As MacDougall remarks, his "work during the months of the Vatican Council represented his final great effort to save Liberal Catholicism."[62] Afterwards, he began to turn in a different direction. The notion of a distinctively Catholic political theory appeared increasingly ephemeral. His historical researches forced him to the conclusion that, in fact,

> the papacy contrived murder and massacre on the largest and also the most cruel and inhuman scale. They were not only wholesale assassins, but they made the principle of assassination a law of the Christian Church and a condition of salvation.[63]

Ultramontanism, however, sanctified the past crimes of the papacy. Its essence was that "the Pope—or that system of authorities concentrated in him—decides the points on which salvation depends. That principle

[61] Cf., MacDougall, op. cit., p. 95.

[62] Ibid., p. 116.

[63] *Acton's Correspondence*, p. 55.

is rejected by those who believe that it is wrong to tell lies or to commit murder for the good of the Church."[64] But, while such persons might reject Ultramontanism, there was no guarantee that it would not be accepted by the Church as a whole: the history of the Vatican Council could offer Acton no solace in this regard. Here the only hope for checking Papal aggression was the Episcopate, but the bishops had failed completely. Moreover, there was no real appeal from the popes, past or present, to the tradition of the Church. For the tradition was equivocal at best on questions of religious toleration and, furthermore, the popes could influence—and had influenced—that tradition, adding to the weight of some past authorities through canonization. This is what had happened, in Acton's view, to two eminent figures of the past who had sanctioned the killing of innocent Protestants: Saint Charles Borromeo and Saint Pius IV.[65] It was unsafe to link morality to Christianity because, when Christianity appears as an institutionalized, historical force, it was often, so to speak, a hostage to forces which had been almost the incarnation of evil. Too often in the past, conscience had been, not enlightened and strengthened by Christ's Church, but warped by it. The case of the Jesuits is instructive. As Acton put it, "It is this combination of an eager sense of duty, zeal for sacrifice, and love of virtue, with the deadly taint of a conscience perverted by authority, that makes them so odious to touch and so curious to study."[66] Indeed, it was the fact that the Church's influence is directed towards the spiritual realm, the sphere of conscience that had made it the source of a more deadly corruption than that spread either by royal absolutism or by modern revolutionary republicanism: the papacy's corruption is "the fiend skulking behind the Crucifix."[67] By 1879, Acton could count himself with pride among those "who sacrifice ... authority to morality," and in this way fulfill the divine purpose better than its supposed official representatives.[68]

Another indication that what concerned Acton was the part of Christian ethical teaching which it had in common with the teaching of the higher pagan philosophers, with other religions, and with the common sense of mankind, as embodied in the legal codes of virtually all nations,

---

[64] Ibid., p. 42.

[65] It appears that Acton was mistaken in attributing this view to these two men.

[66] *Letters to Mary Gladstone*, p. 114.

[67] *Acton's Correspondence*, p. 56.

[68] Ibid., p. 54.

and not anything distinctively Christian, is contained in his repeated assertion that large portions of traditional Christian morality are outside the historian's legitimate field of interest. (We must, of course, keep in mind that Acton never spoke of the historian without meaning at the same time mankind's judge over the actions of past figures.) He writes that the moral judgment of history "n'est pas celui de la vie privée. Bien des péchés n'influent pas sur la véracité et n'entrent pas en compte, ou n'y entrent que rarement." In the case of Louis XIV, for instance, his disordered private life is of historical significance only because of the biographical fact that, once it ceased, his mania for religious persecution began.[69] Acton points out on another occasion, that "Je mets en avant autant que je puis l'idée de crime au lieu de celle d'erreur et de péché," while complaining that Döllinger never appreciated his position on this.[70]

Finally, the connection between the idea of rights flowing from duties and the question of the religious basis of morality is stated explicitly by Acton:

> although I fully admit that political rights proceed directly from religious duties, and hold this to be the true basis of Liberalism, I do not mean to say that there is no other foundation for a system of rights for men who know of no relation between man and God.[71]

It is, however, difficult to know how much of a concession Acton is making here to non-religious ethical systems. While reaffirming his belief that the natural rights of man derive from religiously-based duties, he is willing to concede that there are other possible bases for these rights—but bases which, presumably, he must hold to be false. We shall indicate the nature of the problem that arises presently, in discussing a similar difficulty in Acton's appreciation of the ethical beliefs of George Eliot.

Two cases will serve to show that Acton eventually came to the conclusion that morality was not inevitably tied to Christianity, nor even to religious faith in general: that of the pre-Christian philosophers, and of his contemporary, George Eliot.

---

[69] Ibid., p. 282.
[70] Ibid., p. 63.
[71] Quoted in Kochan, op. cit., p. 95.

Acton had long been interested in the relationship between the religious thought of antiquity and of Christianity, and at one time considered the plan of writing an essay on the theme. The close approach of ancient ethical thinking at its best to the thought of the Gospels and the early Church was an idea that occurred to him whenever he saw it challenged. He criticized Döllinger, for example, for not having made clear in his *Heidenthum und Judenthum* the actual progress achieved by pagan thinking in the centuries of its predominance; if he had, then the real scope of the innovation represented by Christianity would have been clearer.[72] This he termed "one of the most important problems in the philosophy of history," and he desired to have it ascertained to what extent the ethics of Christianity had been anticipated.[73] On more than one occasion he chastised Gladstone for underestimating the value of the ethical thought of antiquity, and overestimating what Christianity had accomplished for culture and morality. Very significant is Acton's statement that

> it would be very difficult indeed to show that the interval between the Ethics of Seneca and the Ethics of St. Ambrose could never have been bridged over by the progress and combination of Stoic, Alexandrian and Chinese morality, as they stood, apart from the Gospel.[74]

Not only did Acton come to believe that an adequate moral system could be achieved independently of Christianity, but he also concluded that classical philosophy contributed a necessary antidote to some of the evils in the moral teachings of historical Christianity: "Religion alone," one of his manuscript cards read, "is no safeguard for morality. Classical philosophy giving an independent morality prevents men from falling under such teachers as Knox, Beza, and Suarez."[75]

In the case of Acton's attitude towards George Eliot we have an even clearer example of his mature judgment that morality is possible independently of Christianity or of any religion.

Acton's estimate of Eliot was very high, not to say extravagant. He wrote to Mary Gladstone:

---

[72] *Acton's Correspondence*, p. 297.

[73] Ibid., p. 255.

[74] Ibid., p. 264.

[75] Quoted in Kochan, op. cit., pp. 95–96.

> You cannot think how much I owe her. Of eighteen or twenty writers by whom I am conscious that my mind has been formed, she was one.... In problems of life and thought, which baffled Shakespeare disgracefully, her touch was unfailing. No writer ever lived who had anything like her power to manifold, but disinterested and impartially observant sympathy.[76]

The basic reason for the enormous appeal of Eliot to him is sketched in a letter to Lady Blennerhassett, on the occasion of the publication of his article on Eliot in 1885. This appeal, it becomes clear, has chiefly to do with her place in the history of modern atheism.

Over the past 200 years, Acton asserts, atheism has been continually on the rise, until today "about one-half of the classic writing, of the creative thinking of the world [is] done by unbelievers.... No minds could be reared except by the aid of Grote, Mill, Austin, Darwin, Lewis, Huxley, Tyndall, Clifford—to take England only. The universities were saturated with their books."[77]

But in the midst of a situation where atheism was coming, if not absolutely to prevail, at least to present an alternative to belief which a substantial part of the educated class might be expected to embrace, the old question of the possibility of an enduring ethical system based on atheism had not yet been settled. "Many think that no enduring system of moral order can be founded on disbelief in God. Everybody sees that there is no security that the ethics of Infidelity will practically harmonize with the ethics of Belief."[78] In fact, the situation was worse, since the chief atheistic schools of thought—utilitarianism, positivism, pessimism, materialism, etc.—had proven themselves devoid of any ethical system.[79]

It was the great merit of George Eliot to have retrieved this dangerous situation. An atheist taught and surrounded by atheists, her moral teachings, Acton finds, are very elevated. He calls her "a preacher of lofty virtue ... not at all perfect, indeed, or absolutely consistent, but far more impressive, more true, more elevated, than any but the very best Christian writers." She had, he thought, redeemed atheism "from the most formidable and most ancient peril and reproach"—that of being unable

[76] *Letters to Mary Gladstone*, p. 57.
[77] *Acton's Correspondence*, p. 290.
[78] Ibid., p. 289.
[79] Ibid., p. 291.

to sustain a code of morality. In fact, Eliot's new morality was in some respects to be preferred to that of "current religions": "It has no weak places, no evil champions, no bad purpose, no screen or excuse, unlike almost all forms of Christianity."[80] Finally, she seems to have been the harbinger of a strong ethical movement in the agnostic and atheistic camp, so that in the present day, in England and Germany at least, writers such as Hartmann, Spencer, Stephen, Sidgwick, etc., have contributed to the formation of a responsible ethic of unbelief.[81]

It is true that Eliot's moral teachings, because of their atheistic underpinnings, were somewhat superficial. "Deny God, and whole branches of deeper morality lose their sanction. Here I am preaching against Bradlaugh, after all."[82] But there is no reason to believe that Acton is here implying the existence of any disabling condition in Eliot's ethics; it was, presumably, still capable of sustaining a free society, even if certain loftier spheres were closed to it.

Although this would seem to establish Acton's later position on the subject unequivocally, the letter here discussed leaves one somewhat puzzled. In the first place, Acton admits that, in his view, whatever the loftiness of Eliot's teachings, they were basically mistaken, for "the keystone of her philosophy" was the idea of Earthly Retribution: that evildoers, in the nature of things, are punished for their sins and crimes on earth. This is an idea, Acton states, "which no historical-minded person can accept. She herself was aware that virtue is not much happier than crime; and she never filled up this tremendous gap." That it is also an idea which "goes down so well with British Christians,"[83] seems rather unimportant in the long run, if, as Acton states, it is plainly false, for her atheistic ethical system is then one which cannot possibly hope to endure.

Moreover, Acton's claim that Bentham and Mill were "destitute of any ethical system" would indicate that he had not devoted any substantial amount of analytical thought to the subject. Presumably this judgment is a reflection of his distaste for any form of the pleasure philosophy, his belief that pleasure and pain are irrelevant to the categories of ethics (we have already encountered this idea in the case of Constant); but then he

[80]Ibid., pp. 291–292.
[81]Ibid., p. 291.
[82]*Letters to Mary Gladstone*, p. 96.
[83]*Acton's Correspondence*, p. 292.

would seem to be ignoring the possibilities of a more elevated morality contained in Mill's distinction between higher and lower pleasures; and, furthermore, it is difficult to see why, on this basis, he should regard as legitimate the ethics of Spencer and Sidgwick.

It must be admitted, therefore, that Acton's position on Eliot leaves some room for confusion as to his view of the connection between unbelief and morality—and hence between unbelief and freedom. We may conclude, nevertheless, that the mature Acton had definitely rejected what he referred to in a letter to Döllinger as "das Vorurteil das es keine Sicherheit für die Tugend gibt ohne Gott,"[84] and that there is little evidence for the claim advanced in a recent work on Acton and John Henry Newman: "Though differing considerably in their approach to many questions, they were agreed that only in religious culture could freedom flourish."[85]

Acton's view of the relationship between religion and freedom can be made considerably clearer if we examine how he conceived these two factors to have interacted in history.

This is the predominant theme of the great History of Liberty to which he devoted so much thinking and planning. Although, of course, he never completed or even really began it, the vision is discernibly present in his two lectures, "The History of Freedom in Antiquity" and "The History of Freedom in Christianity,"[86] and in his review of Erskine May's *Democracy in Europe*;[87] these essays, supplemented by other pertinent material, may justly be taken as reflecting more or less his mature judgment on religion's historical relationship to liberty.

From the very beginning of the first of these, Acton presents the course of liberty through history as slow, hard and devious. At all times, it has had to make its way against its natural enemies, "ignorance, superstition … lust of conquest and love of ease … the strong man's craving for power, and the poor man's craving for food."[88] But, as Tocqueville believed that Providence was leading the world towards equality, Acton held that the

[84] Quoted in Woodward, loc. cit., p. 264.
[85] MacDougall, op. cit., p. ix.
[86] *Freedom and Power*, pp. 53–112.
[87] *History of Freedom*, pp. 61–100.
[88] *Freedom and Power*, p. 53.

finger of God is discernible in the world's progress to freedom; he speaks of "the methods by which divine wisdom has educated the nations to appreciate and to assume the duties of freedom." For Acton, the idea that something more than human intention is involved in the unfolding of liberty in history was not purely rhetorical; this may be gathered from the fact that, while he believed that liberty had to a large extent been established by his day in the Anglo-Saxon nations, "at all times, sincere friends of freedom have been rare, and its triumphs have been due to minorities, that have prevailed by associating themselves with auxiliaries whose objects often differed from their own."[89] Thus, while history may be looked on as the history of freedom, and while freedom has forced its way to a relative triumph, peculiarly, at every point, it has been the goal of only a small minority; and interests and parties whose objects have been far different, and even contrary, have unintentionally contributed to its growth.[90] Acton here posits something like an invisible hand, operating throughout history, conducing to the victory of liberal ideas and institutions. And the "invisible hand" for Acton, unlike as for Smith, is not simply a euphemism for certain empirically observable forces in the social organization making for unintentional order. He severely criticized Newman, for instance, for denying "the divine government of the world," for believing that "Providence does not manifest itself in history," that "the law of Progress is not the law of history."[91] To Döllinger he asserted:

> there is a grand unity in the history of ideas—of conscience, or morality, and of the means of securing it. I venture to say that the secret of the philosophy of History lies there:—It is the only point of view from which one discovers a constant progress, the only one therefore which justifies the ways of God to man.[92]

This progress towards freedom is not merely a generalization which holds for the past: it can be expected to continue indefinitely. Here Acton's

---

[89] Ibid.

[90] Compare Tocqueville on democracy: "all men have aided it by their exertions, both those who have intentionally labored in its cause and those who have served it unwittingly; those who have fought for it and even those who have declared themselves its opponents have all been driven along in the same direction, have all labored to one end ... [it] is, therefore, a providential fact." *Democracy in America*, vol. 1, p. 6.

[91] Quoted in MacDougall, op. cit., p. 175.

[92] Ibid., p. 169.

thinking begins to touch on millenarianism and utopianism: one of his manuscript notes reads: "End with the Kingdom of God, which is liberty."[93]

But given that religion in the sense just outlined forms the core of Acton's philosophy of history, what more specifically does history show to have been its connection with the growth of liberty?

In the first place, there is no positive connection between religion per se and freedom, and certainly religion is not a sufficient condition for a free society. Indeed, the religious beliefs and ecclesiastical organization of a society may operate in a fashion decidedly detrimental to liberty. In addition to the cases of the Russian Church and the Russian State, and Islam and the Islamic states, the best example of this principle are the states of classical antiquity. Here it was precisely the religious beliefs of the people which reinforced the essentially totalitarian thrust of their political organization.

This is a theme which is in many ways crucial for Acton's conception. The great value he placed on the Catholic Church as a liberating factor in history can only be fully justified given his interpretation of the essential nature of the classical state. We need not, however, examine in detail his account of the constitutional crises and evolution of the Athenian and Roman polities. It will be sufficient to point up the lessons which Acton suggests may be gained from this evolution.

While the Greek contribution of democracy represented in several respects an advance for the cause of freedom, the Athenian experiment failed on account of both institutional and ideological flaws (corresponding to the two levels on which Acton pursues this theme in these essays). On the one hand, there existed no real division of powers, no system of checks and balances, for the "humblest and most numerous class of Athenians united the legislative, the judicial and, in part, the executive." Moreover,

> the philosophy that was then in the ascendant taught them that there is no law superior to that of the State—the law-giver is above the law. It followed that the sovereign people had a right to do whatever was within its power, and was bound by no rule of right or wrong, but its own judgment of expediency ... the emancipated people of Athens became a tyrant.[94]

[93]Ibid., p. 173.

[94]*Freedom and Power*, pp. 63–64.

The same basic flaw is to be found in the Roman state, and the true nature of the classical polity is as follows:

> [The ancients] concentrated so many prerogatives in the State as to leave no footing from which a man could deny its jurisdiction or assign bounds to its activity.... The vice of the classic State was that it was both Church and State in one. Morality was undistinguished from religion and politics from morals; and in religion morality and politics there was only one legislator and one authority. The State ... claimed the use of all [man's] faculties and the determination of all his duties.... What the slave was in the hands of his master, the citizen was in the hands of the community. The most sacred obligations vanished before the public advantage.[95]

This is a highly important passage, and we will return to an analysis of it; we ought to observe, however, that Acton is here continuing the traditional nineteenth-century liberal interpretation of the nature of the classical state that we have already encountered in the thought of Constant, Laboulaye and others. Its chief significance lies in the fact that, by depicting the ancient republics as by law and ethos virtual totalitarian states, it raises the question: What was responsible for the transformation of the view of the relation between state and citizen? While Constant, as we have seen, traces it to various social factors, such as population, the degree of militarism of the two civilizations, etc., many of the later authors sought the key in the religion whose emergence and triumph marked off the two epochs. It is this tradition to which Acton attaches himself.

In Acton's view, totalitarianism is not merely the final outcome of the politics of the ancient world: it permeated much of it from the beginning. Thus, in the case of the early Roman Republic, he ascribed the acceptance of human sacrifice on the part of the populace to their idolatrous attitude towards the State: "The deification of the State made every sacrifice which it exacted seem as nothing in comparison with the fortune of Rome; and the perils which for centuries menaced it from Carthage or Gaul, Epirus or Pontus, Parthia, Spain or Germany, each demanded its human victims."[96] By the end of the classical period, whatever breath of freedom had existed was extinguished: "love and appreciation of liberty were absorbed by

[95] Ibid., pp. 68–69.

[96] Quoted in Lally, op. cit., p. 220.

respect for law, so that at the time of the Teutonic invasions the latter alone survived."[97]

If we return to the lengthy passage quoted above, we find two elements which may be separated out in the state worship of antiquity. First, the recognized claims of the state were limitless, and there was, so to speak, no Archimedean point outside of it from which the individual might reject them. The highest law acknowledged was that of the general welfare, and no individual obligations or duties could be suffered to stand in its way. Second, and reinforcing the first, was the fact that morality and religion were both branches of politics. The gods were national gods, and their function was to preserve the state. It mattered not at all whether the sovereign was the *demos*, as at Athens, or, as in the later history of Rome, the emperor who governed in the name and supposed interest of the *demos*: classical democracy and classical imperial absolutism were both grounded in the same totalitarian view of the omnipotence of the state and the insignificance of the individual.

While religion in classical times afforded no aid to liberty, but rather the reverse, there did finally emerge a religion that has assisted the growth of freedom mightily, that may actually be said to have founded freedom. This is Roman Catholicism.[98]

If God's purpose in history is the progressive emergence and establishment of liberty, it is scarcely surprising that he should have taken advantage of His Church to promote His ends. But what precisely was Catholicism's contribution to liberty? If we were to judge solely by the actions of the early Church, Acton asserts, precious little. Significantly, he uses the idea of passive obedience to a despot as a touchstone in this matter. Although the early Christian writers were not unanimous on the subject, and Origen "spoke with approval of conspiring for the destruction of tyranny," the weight of the authority of the early church seems to have been on the side of acquiescence by the subject in whatever the civil power might choose to do.[99] It was only with time and suitable circumstances that certain liberal implications of the New Testament manifested themselves.

---

[97] Ibid., pp. 139–140.

[98] Although Acton speaks in terms of Christianity in these essays, it will become clear that what he has in mind is essentially the Roman Catholic form.

[99] *Freedom and Power*, pp. 79–60.

These implications did *not* have to do with the *rationale* for liberty. The term "liberty" and similar expressions are employed a number of times in the New Testament. Thus: "The truth shall make you free" (John 8:32); "Free from the law of sin and death" (Romans 8:2); "Where the spirit of the Lord is, there is liberty" (II Cor. 3:17); etc. It is most significant that Acton chose to ignore these passages, and concentrated instead on a different passage (which does not contain the term "liberty"). It strongly indicates that Acton was aware that the New Testament references to liberty, freedom, etc., had no direct bearing on his subject; they referred, rather, to a metaphysical and theological conception.[100] As far as the Gospels, St. Paul, etc., are concerned, civil liberty—the subject with which Acton was dealing—was of little or no importance.

Acton makes it clear that Christianity did not importantly add to the body of philosophical arguments for freedom. "There is hardly a truth in politics or in the system of rights of man that was not grasped by the wisest of the Gentiles and the Jews, or that they did not declare with a refinement of thought and a nobleness of expression that later writers could never surpass."[101] The Stoics, especially, had already come upon the keystone of the arch of liberty, the doctrine of the higher law. It was they "who emancipated mankind from its subjection to despotic rule." This they achieved by making

> it known that there is a will superior to the collective will of man, and a law that overrules those of Solon and Lycurgus. Their test of good government is its conformity to principles that can be traced to a higher legislator. That which we must obey, that to which we are bound to reduce all civil authorities, and to sacrifice every earthly interest, is that immutable law which is perfect and eternal as God Himself, which proceeds from his nature, and reigns over heaven and earth and over all nations.[102]

In this way, Stoicism made good the chief philosophical impediment to the advance of liberty in classical times and the flaw which had condemned

[100]Cf., Pieter Geyl, "The Idea of Liberty in History," in *Encounters in History* (New York: Meridian, 1961), p. 245. Acton explicitly makes this distinction in a letter to Mary Gladstone: "[I]t is wrong, in a political book, to call Luther an apostle of freedom, as he was an apostle of authority and divine right, and promoted freedom in the other, the spiritual sense." *Letters to Mary Gladstone*, p. 192.

[101]*Freedom and Power*, p. 79.

[102]Ibid., p. 76.

Athenian democracy, for instance, to failure.[103]

Moreover, on the institutional level, there had existed mixed governments, and popular ones, and ones based on a federal structure. What had been lacking was *effectively limited* governments; there was "no State the circumference of whose authority had been defined by a force external to its own."[104] In this pregnant passage, we can discern the fruit of Acton's reflections on power. He had agreed with Montesquieu and Calhoun (among others) that the tendency to abuse power and to enlarge it at the expense of others is a constituent part of human nature. For this reason, the doctrine of checks and balances and the division of powers (particularly including federalism) is the foundation of the liberal theory of state organization. "Liberty," Acton maintained, "depends on the division of power."[105] This doctrine attempts to divide up the powers at the disposal of the state among its various branches, in the expectation that in this way the will to power of one branch will be held in check by that of others, preventing total control from being exercised by one will. So far, however, nothing is achieved for the goal of limiting the *whole collection* of state powers. This cannot be done by anybody which is part of the state apparatus, and some force external to the state would somehow have to be induced to assume the task.

That this had never been the case in antiquity was responsible for the fact that the limits of state power had remained largely philosophical and ideal:

> Those who proclaimed the assistance of a higher authority had indeed drawn a metaphysical barrier before the governments, but they had not known how to make it real. [The Stoics, for instance,] could only advise the wise to hold aloof from politics, keeping the unwritten law in his heart.[106]

This situation was radically changed by Christianity, and the key scriptural passage here is Jesus's admonition to "Render unto Caesar the things that

[103] It is, however, open to Acton to maintain—although he does not do so, at least explicitly—that, while the doctrine of the higher law was not discovered by the Church, the latter was responsible for incorporating it into the structure of its religious beliefs, and thus giving it a much wider currency that it could have attained as the dogma of a merely philosophical school.

[104] Ibid., pp. 80–81.

[105] *Letters to Mary Gladstone*, p. 98.

[106] *Freedom and Power*, p. 81.

are Caesar's and unto God the things that are God's." These words, in Acton's view,

> gave the civil power, under the protection of conscience, a sacredness it had never enjoyed and bounds it had never acknowledged; and they were the repudiation of absolutism and the inauguration of freedom.[107]

The great advance represented by the Christian version of this idea over, say, the Stoic one, consisted in the fact that it was not merely the product of a chain of moral reasoning or of the insight of a sage, but that Jesus "created the force to execute it."

> To maintain the necessary immunity in one supreme sphere, to reduce all political authority within defined limits, ceased to be an aspiration of patient reasoners, and was made the perpetual charge and care of the most energetic and the most universal association in the world.[108]

This was the root from which grew liberty as Western Europe was to know it. As Acton expressed it on another occasion: "All liberty consists *in radice* in the preservation of an inner sphere exempt from State power. That reverence for conscience is the germ of all civil freedom, and the way in which Christianity served it ... liberty has grown out of the distinction (separation is a bad word) of Church and State."[109]

The great merit of Christianity, then, was to have arranged things such that (a) there would exist a very powerful extra-state force, and (b) this force would find itself in collision with the state. Thus, one area, at least, of human action (and, indeed, the most important area) had been removed from the control of the state, whether democratic or not, and a powerful institution had been made its trustee: there had been created the term of what Acton had once earlier referred to as "the hierarchical organization,

---

[107] Ibid. As we have seen, Laboulaye also makes this passage the pivot of his discussion of the same issue. Fustel de Coulanges likewise emphasizes its importance, op. cit., p. 393. More recently, Ernest Barker has followed Acton's judgment on the extreme importance of this passage, as well as his analysis of the impact of Christianity, and especially of the medieval papacy, on liberty; see his *Principles of Social and Political Theory* (Oxford: Oxford University, 1961), pp. 7–11.

[108] *Freedom and Power*, p. 81.

[109] *Acton and His Circle*, p. 254.

which renders Catholicism so formidable to statesmen."[110] That the limits of this area outside of state control would be in dispute, and that in any case, the wielders of political power would be vexed by the very existence of such an area, would in the future provide cause for beneficent conflict between the two authorities.

Before tracing the historical operation of the principle just outlined, however, two important points must be underscored.

First, Acton emphasizes that it was certainly not the conscious intention of the Catholic Church to promote liberty. As an institution, it was scarcely more devoted to free institutions than was the state power itself. At times, to be sure, it seemed to aid freedom from disinterested motives, as when, in the early Middle Ages, the clergy "taught that power ought to be conferred by election; and the Councils of Toledo furnished the framework of the parliamentary system of Spain, which is, by a long interval, the oldest in the world."[111] At other times, however, it has acted in a manner distinctly contrary to the interests of liberty, as when, in the seventeenth century, it supported the idea of the divine right of kings. But this should give little cause for wonder. The hierarchy of the Church is, of course, composed of human beings, and there is no reason to suppose—certainly none, if the matter is viewed historically—that these men will be any more able to escape the innate human striving for power than will other men. The assistance which the Church furnished to liberty was motivated by selfish interest. As we shall see, the struggle against the Empire and the other European monarchies, which begins with Hildebrand, was one of self-defense; with popes such as Boniface VIII, the Church gave itself over to an aspiration for universal monarchy dominion over the political order, and, as Acton put it, "sought to substitute a despotism of priests for the tyranny of kings."[112]

The second point that must be made is that Acton's view of the assistance given liberty by the Catholic Church is a "naturalistic" one. That is, although he was, of course, of the belief that it was the Church founded

[110]Quoted in MacDougall, op. cit., p. 71.

[111]*Freedom and Power*, pp. 85–86.

[112]Quoted in Kochan, op. cit., pp. 50–51.

by Christ and a uniquely divine institution, when he comes to explain how it acted to promote liberty, the explanation contains no reference to these facts. Acton's explanation could be accepted in its entirety by a non-Catholic, a non-Christian, or even an atheist, since it deals in terms of social and political forces which are brought into existence and interact with one another in a purely non-supernatural way. It is the eye of Acton the believer, not of Acton the historian, which discerns the finger of God in the march of freedom through history.

If the Christian epoch is dated from the establishment of Christianity as the official religion of the Empire, then it is from the very beginning of this epoch that the fruitful struggle of Church and State dates. In the nature of things, it was the state which was the aggressor, and Constantine as well as his successors attempted by every means at their disposal to turn the Church into "the gilded crutch of absolutism." Despite his conversion to Christianity, he fully intended to carry forward Diocletian's attempt to found a despotism of the Asiatic type, even aiming to make use of Christianity for this purpose. Acton suggests, for instance, that moving the seat of government to the East was part of the Emperor's plan to remove his Church from the influence of the Roman patriarch, and found a patriarchate that would be absolutely under his control.[113]

At first—as was again to be the case during the Reformation—divisions within Christianity helped absolutism along by dividing the possible opponents of the state and even inducing them to look to the civil power for support against their theological enemies.[114] Thus, Acton implies, a situation of countervailing powers, rather than one in which a fragmented Church faces a unified state was, at least at this point in history, most conducive to liberty.

Ecclesiastical resistance to state pretentions during the early centuries was further impeded by the traditions of state worship deriving from the late Empire and of political quietism handed down from the early Christians. During the earlier Middle Ages the Church entered into a sort of bargain with the barbarian kings, exchanging the means of conducting

[113] *Freedom and Power*, pp. 82–83.
[114] Ibid., p. 83.

government—the knowledge at the disposal of its relatively well-educated clergy—for special exemptions.[115] This was a time of civilization and state building, of the taming and Christianizing of the barbarians, and it was not to be expected that freedom would flourish under these conditions.

It was only with the emergence of high feudalism that the conflict that was to be so productive for liberty began to develop. This was a time when

> the nations of the West lay between the competing tyrannies of local magnates and of absolute monarchs, when a force was brought upon the scene which proved for a time superior to the vassal and his lord.[116]

In the history of European freedom, this era was the crucial one. The Normans had destroyed the liberties of England, and the primitive democratic institutions of the barbarians had fallen into decay, while the towns and the middle class had not yet come onto the scene:

> The only influence capable of resisting the feudal hierarchy was the ecclesiastical hierarchy; and they came into collision, when the process of feudalism threatened the independence of the Church by subjecting prelates severally to that form of personal dependence on the kings which was peculiar to the Teutonic State.[117]

The importance of the Investiture Controversy is emphasized by Acton: "To that conflict of four hundred years we owe the rise of civil liberty,"[118] and there will develop "a long tradition [connecting] the Hildebrandine controversy with the Long Parliament, and St. Thomas with Edmund Burke."[119] This is the prime example of Acton's whole theme, and the chief way in which Christianity has historically aided the progress of liberty.

The promotion of liberty was no part of the intention of either kings or popes in this struggle; just as St. Thomas, the leading Guelph writer, "would have made the papacy control all Christian governments," so Marsilius of Padua would have subjected the clergy to the civil power. Liberty was rather "the means by which the temporal and the spiritual power called

[115]Ibid., p. 85.
[116]Ibid., p. 86.
[117]Ibid.
[118]Ibid.
[119]Ibid., p. 97.

the nations to their aid."[120] In their attempt to draw allies to their side, the papacy and the monarchies were forced to make concessions to the people on both the theoretical and institutional levels. Institutionally, as a result of the conflict, "the towns of Italy and Germany won their franchises, France got her States-General, and England her Parliament out of the alternate phases of the contest." As long as it lasted, the struggle forestalled the rise of the doctrine of divine right. Political theory set limits to the legitimate action of kings, and it came to be commonly held that there existed "a public law to which all monarchs were held subject." It was in accordance with this conception that King John, for instance, was brought to account. By the thirteenth century, both Guelphs and Ghibellines were admitting what was essentially the Whig theory of government, and Acton refers to St. Thomas as the "first Whig."[121]

How the Church acted to prevent the rise of the sort of absolutism that had marked the late Roman Empire and had since become entrenched at Constantinople is illustrated by the following:

> A disposition existed to regard the Crown as an estate descending under the law of real property in the family that possessed it. But the authority of religion, and especially the papacy, was thrown on the side that denied the indefeasible title of kings.[122]

Thus it was while acting mainly in its own interest that the Church promoted the interests of liberty. The Church upheld the notion that a people had the right to deprive their king of his throne under certain conditions; gradually (presumably in accordance with its own inner logic), this idea "was made to stand on broader grounds, and was strong enough to resist both Church and State."[123]

The readiness of the people to stand up to their kings was strengthened by the Church's chronic undermining of the dignity of royalty. The people were "accustomed to see those whom they most respected [the clergy]

---

[120]Ibid., p. 87. Acton makes the same point in his review of Erskine May's *Democracy in Europe*, using the term "democracy" (but it is clear that he is speaking of the same development as above): "Christianity did not directly influence political progress.... The revival of democracy was due neither to the Christian Church nor to the Teutonic State, but to the quarrel between them." *History of Freedom*, pp. 79–80.

[121]*Freedom and Power*, pp. 87–89.

[122]Ibid., p. 87.

[123]Ibid.

in constant strife with their rulers," and distrust of the civil power was promoted by popes such as Gregory VII, who referred to states as the work of the devil. In such an atmosphere it was quite unlikely that there should arise any analogue to the emperor worship of antiquity.

What Acton conceived to be the principle operating here may be fathered from his comment on certain Austrian concessions to the papacy in his own time:

> now that Francis Joseph has publicly acknowledged the rights of the Pope in matters hitherto belonging to the State, will not his subjects ask themselves whether perchance in other respects, too, the State has not hitherto overstepped the limits of its just authority? No State is safe from the influence of so pernicious an example.[124]

That is, special rights wrested from the state by a powerful Church not only remove certain areas from state control directly, but provide an example and precedent for the acquisition of other privileges by non-ecclesiastical agencies. By virtue of its character as a corporation "strong enough for resistance, permanent in its organization, constant in its maxims, and superior to national boundaries," the Church was enabled to become the first body to acquire those privileges and special rights which are the characteristic of medieval liberty.[125]

Acton sums up the achievements of the Middle Ages from the point of view for freedom, which were much more impressive than is commonly believed. While he states that they were not so much "towards the perfection of their institutions" as "towards the attaining of the knowledge of political truth," there are two highly significant institutional changes which he mentions, both signaling great advances over the state of affairs at the end of the classical period: first, representative bodies had become almost universal, and second, slavery had virtually disappeared. On the theoretical level, there was general recognition that no "tax was lawful that was not granted by the class that paid for it," and—a theme that was central for Acton—"the right of insurrection was not only admitted, but defined, as a duty sanctioned by religion."[126]

Comparing the medieval with the classical period, Acton declares:

---

[124] *Lord Acton and His Circle*, p. 94.

[125] Quoted in Kochan, op. cit., pp. 50–51.

[126] *Freedom and Power*, p. 91.

> The issue of ancient politics was an absolute state planted on slavery. The political produce of the Middle Ages was a system of states in which authority was restricted by the representation of powerful classes, by privileged associations, and by the acknowledgment of duties superior to those which are imposed by man.[127]

While much remained to be done in practice, "the great problems of principle had been solved."[128]

Nevertheless, as Acton points out, there existed a certain provincialism in medieval Christianity which had a deleterious effect on liberty. It had been held that, true religion being of supreme importance, the rights of man—the duties of their neighbors and rulers towards them—varied according to their religion. This was not, of course, a doctrine implied in Christianity as a system of ideas which may be gathered from the New Testament; rather, it was part of the system of ideas and sentiments associated with historical Christianity. Nevertheless, it proved useful to the modern state (which emerges from about the fourteenth century), by promoting some of the latter's more objectionable claims. And not only was this denial of the rule of law taken over by the state as against *its* enemies, but the idea was to have very unfortunate consequences once the religious unity of Europe was fragmented by the Reformation.[129]

The sixteenth century represented in every way a retrogression for liberty. A process had been underway by which both monarch's power was increasing in fact, and his claims were being widened in theory. The role that the Catholic Church had previously filled, that of acting as a counterweight to the civil power, fell into abeyance. Here Acton indicates that the reason is largely to be sought in the failure of the Conciliar movement, which, with its attempt to create a sort of constitutional monarchy in the Church, posed a threat to the power of the popes, uniting them to the kings in opposition to "the system of divided authority." In addition, in France, Spain, Sicily and England, strong monarchs were able to bring the Church under their control, and thus demolish the delicate balance of Church and State which had previously provided a free area in which other social bodies might flourish.[130]

---

[127] Ibid.
[128] Ibid.
[129] Ibid., pp. 91–92.
[130] Ibid., p. 93.

Thus the tide was already running strongly in the direction of absolutism when the Reformation broke out.

Acton's views on the Reformation are particularly important for our subject, since this is the point at which it becomes clearest that, unlike Constant and Tocqueville, Acton is emphasizing the contribution not of the religious sentiment or of Christianity as a whole, but of Roman Catholicism.[131]

Prima facie one would have expected that Luther's influence would have worked against the absolutist tendencies of the sixteenth century, since he was faced with a strong alliance of Church and State, and, in fact, his most determined enemies at first were to be found within the political and not the ecclesiastical structure. Unfortunately, it was otherwise. First, because "the dread of revolution was the deepest of [Luther's] political sentiments," and the obsequiousness of this priest towards the state went so far, in Acton's view, that he may justly be called the inventor of the theory of the divine right of kings. Secondly, because of his radical rejection of the medieval heritage of Christianity and his desire to return the Church to the pristine Apostolic age, Luther was led to reject also the liberal achievements of the medieval period and the scholastic writers.[132]

We have seen that Acton thought that the Gospels and the early Church manifested a relative lack of interest in liberty; it was under the pressure of actual conflict with a self-aggrandizing political power that the seed of liberty contained in Jesus's injunction germinated. Luther, therefore, with his too literal interpretation of the New Testament and his rejection of Church tradition, was condemned to accept "the passive obedience of the apostolic age" and could not agree with the "gloss by which the Guelphic

[131] The contrary doctrine that it was Protestantism, as against Catholicism, that was conducive to freedom and crucial in its historical development was, of course, a widespread one in the nineteenth century (it constituted, for example, part of the Whig interpretation of history) and can be traced to the Enlightenment. Thomas Erskine May, for instance, maintained that the historian could "observe despotism allied to Pagan superstitions and corruptions of the Christian faith" and "liberty flourishing in union with the best and purest types of Christianity"; and in this connection he cites Montesquieu, who in *L'esprit des lois* (bk. 4, chap. 5) states: "Les peuples du nord embrassèrent le protestantisme, et ceux du midi la catholique." "C'est que les peuples du nord ont et auront toujours un esprit d'indépendance et de liberté, que n'ont pas les peuples du midi." *Democracy in Europe* (New York: Middleton, 1879), p. xxv.

[132] Ibid., p. 94.

divines had got over" it, since this "was characteristic of the medieval method of interpretation which he rejected."[133] It is likely that Acton had in mind here primarily the famous passage from Romans 13:1–2. For him, as is evident throughout these essays, the assertion of the right of insurrection and the denial of passive obedience was of paramount importance. Thus, virtually his only mention of Zwingli's political views in this lecture has to do with the fact that, compared to Luther, he at least had the virtue of not shrinking from "the medieval idea that evil magistrates must be cashiered."[134] But the brevity of his reforming career forestalled any profound influence by Zwingli on the political ideas of the Reformation.

Calvin, too, accomplished nothing for liberty; on the contrary, he was a determined opponent of popular institutions, and "desired an aristocracy of the elect, armed with the means of punishing not only crime, but vice and error"—in short, a theocracy. Again, as with Luther, his chief mistake consisted in sweeping away the achievements of the Middle Ages in favor of an older tradition—this time, the theocratic tradition of Hebrews. In this way, Calvin undid the great accomplishment of medieval Christianity in forcing a distinction between the realms of Church and State; he returned to what was in form the pagan state, with the difference that it was the spiritual order which now engulfed the secular.[135]

This is merely another instance of what Acton takes to be the general character of the period of the Renaissance and Reformation: it is a time that was signalized by the disappearance in many areas of the highly beneficial division of powers between Church and State. By his hatred of antiauthoritarian impulses and movements, and by depriving them of effective strength through his approval of the idea of passive obedience, Luther virtually subjected the Church to the political authority. It is interesting to note that Acton saw an analogous development in the Renaissance Church. At one time he had wanted to make clear "the connection between the absolutist tendencies of the Church [at the time of Julius II and Leo X] and the establishment of the Roman monarchy [the temporal power], which

[133] Ibid. Another example of Acton's emphasis on this principle is that of Socinus, who, he states, "was the first who on grounds that Church and State ought to be separated required universal toleration. But Socinus disarmed his own theory, for he was a strict advocate of passive obedience." Ibid., p. 104. (Italics added.)

[134] Ibid., p. 94.

[135] Ibid., p. 94. See also, *Lord Acton and His Circle*, pp. 49–50.

is very important and not understood."[136] The growth of the temporal power of the papacy, indeed, introduced a principle not basically distinct from that of the pagan state: "The domain of conscience [is] not distinct, therefore, from the domain of the State—sins, crimes, and sins against faith, even when private, without proselytism, are acts of treason."[137]

Summing up, Acton states that the "direct political influence of the Reformation effected less than has been supposed," largely, presumably, because the direction in which it did affect affairs was the one in which they had already been tending. Indirectly, however, it led to a great increase of state power. The fact of religious schism and heresy was used by rulers already interested in increasing their power to assume "every prerogative needed to preserve their faith," and they were encouraged in this by their people. Thus:

> All the care to keep Church and State asunder and to prevent the confusion of their powers which had been the work of ages, was renounced in the intensity of the struggle.[138]

Acton stresses that religion was the *excuse* employed by princes for their own ends: "all through the religious conflict policy kept the upper hand."

> When the last of the Reformers died, religion, instead of emancipating the nations, had become an excuse for the criminal art of despots. Calvin preached and Bellarmine lectured, but Machiavelli reigned.[139]

In the later sixteenth and the early seventeenth century, however, there occurred the rebirth of the idea of the right of armed resistance to tyranny as a consequence of the religious disunity of Europe. This was provoked by events such as the St. Bartholomew Massacre, and was used to justify the revolt of the Netherlands from Spain.[140] Gradually, the *rationale* for this idea was widened: from being linked to the defense of the "true" religion (which had to vary, of course, from case to case), it came to be founded on natural law and the rights of man. In this sense, Grotius performed a great service. By breaking the connection between natural law and theology, he

---

[136] Quoted in Lally, op. cit., p. 200.

[137] *Lord Acton and His Circle*, p. 256.

[138] *Freedom and Power*, pp. 94–95.

[139] Ibid., pp. 95–96.

[140] Ibid., pp. 96–97.

afforded a basis for the idea of the rights of all men against all oppressive governments, and, as Acton put it, "drew the lines of real political science."

> From that time it became possible to make politics a matter of principle and conscience, so that men and nations differing in all other things could live in peace together, under the sanctions of the common law.[141]

Thus, in this case it is the *separation* of political theory from any moorings in theology or religion to which Acton attributes responsibility for a progress towards freedom.

On the other hand, the seventeenth century also saw liberty promoted by groups that emphasized its close connection with Christian principles. The Independent sects required and demanded religious freedom, and understood that this could only be attained by limiting state power generally. On the whole, Acton assigns religion the greatest weight as a factor leading to the growth of freedom in England in this period:

> [The] great political ideas, sanctifying freedom to God, teaching men to treasure the liberties of others as their own, and to defend them for the love of justice and charity more than as a claim of right, has been the soul of what is great and good in the progress of the last two hundred years. The cause of religion, even under the unregenerated influence of worldly passion, had as much to do as any clear notions of policy in making this country the foremost of the free. It had been the deepest current in the movement of 1641, and it remained the strongest motive that survived the reaction of 1660.[142]

Complementary to his emphasis on religion as a source of inspiration for freedom is Acton's disdain for the argument for liberty based on a defense of property rights. He speaks of Locke, for instance, as one "whose notion of liberty involves nothing more spiritual than the security of property,"[143] and, further on, he writes of the unfortunate effects of Locke's thinking on succeeding writers: "Even Hume did not enlarge the bounds of his ideas; and his narrow materialistic belief in the connection between liberty and

---

[141] Ibid., p. 98.
[142] Ibid., p. 104.
[143] Ibid.

property captivated even the bolder mind of Fox."[144]

In the case of the American Revolution—in Acton's view the most important modern occurrence related to his theme—no special religious motive or influence is emphasized, nor is irreligion held responsible for the failure of the French Revolution. In both cases, however, commitment to the doctrine of the higher law, whether religiously based or not (or lack of such commitment), is seen as crucial to the success or failure of the revolution from a liberal point of view.[145]

Acton does not pursue his subject, in these essays, further than the period of the French Revolution. If he had, his later writings indicate that he would have attributed more weight to liberalism as a coherent movement, and devoted more attention both to its workings out in the later eighteenth and early nineteenth centuries, and to its historical roots. This is of great importance for the questions we are examining, since Acton became convinced that liberalism as a whole was at best unitarian or deist, often agnostic or atheist; generally, he pointed out, the liberal was characterized by an "extreme profaneness of mind."[146] To Gladstone, who had insisted on the supreme importance of belief in the divine nature of Christ for the upward development of culture, Acton retorted by mentioning

> a Church whose Fathers are the later Milton and the later Penn, Locke and Bayle, Toland, Franklin, Turgot, Smith, Washington, Jefferson, Bentham, D. Stewart, Romilly, Jeffrey, B. Constant, Tocqueville [n.b.], Channing, Macaulay, Mill, ... These men and others like them disbelieved that Doctrine, established freedom, and undid the work of orthodox Christianity. They swept away that appalling edifice of intolerance, tyranny, cruelty, which believers in Christ built up, to perpetuate their belief.[147]

Thus, as a practical matter, religious liberty, so crucial in Acton's view for liberty in general, was brought into existence not by the established and orthodox Christian churches, but by writers and statesmen who ranged from unitarians to atheists.

---

[144] Ibid., pp. 105–106. It is interesting that Acton speaks of economic liberalism almost not at all; the only connection in which political economy is cited is that its "sudden rise ... suggested the idea of applying the methods of science to the art of government."

[145] Ibid., pp. 106–108.

[146] *Acton's Correspondence*, p. 49.

[147] Ibid., pp. 216–217.

Ultimately, therefore, the historical relation between Christianity and freedom has been ambiguous. On the one hand, freedom was promoted by the Catholic Church in earlier times, especially in the high Middle Ages. On the other hand, "if Liberalism has a desperate foe it is the Church, as it was in the West, between 1200 and 1600 or 1700." Later Christianity acted in an "anti-liberal and anti-social" manner, until the promotion of liberty was taken up by the independent sects, which in significant ways cannot be identified with historical Christianity, and by non-Christian and anti-Christian forces.[148]

[148]Ibid., p. 217.

CHAPTER 4

Conclusions

Among the most interesting pages of Tocqueville's little masterpiece, *L'Ancien Régime et la Revolution*, are those which he devotes to liberal thought in the decades preceding 1789. He takes the Physiocrats as the group of Enlightenment reformers who most genuinely reflect the underlying principles and tendencies of the age, and passes in review their notions on government and society. Tocqueville notes that they were enemies of institutional limitations on governmental power, trusting to the education of the people in Physiocratic principles to act as an adequate replacement for "solid political guarantees of the nation's freedom." Most interesting is the connection which Tocqueville draws between these writers and the early socialists, particularly in regard to their admiration of a powerful government in the hands of enlightened reformers aiming at the conscious and scientific restructuring of society and even of human nature itself.[1]

We have already noted the sense in which Constant was an opponent of many of the guiding principles of the eighteenth century. Acton, too, takes a similar stand on the subject, and in words which recall Tocqueville's, he states:

[1] *Old Régime*, pp. 157–164.

> all these factions of opinion [in pre-Revolutionary France] were called Liberal: Montesquieu, because he was an intelligent Tory; Voltaire, because he attacked the clergy; Turgot, as a reformer; Rousseau, as a democrat; Diderot, as a freethinker. The one thing in common to them all is the disregard for liberty.[2]

Their remarks on this point are indicative of the fact that for all three liberals we have considered in these pages, the experience of France and of Europe after 1789 demonstrated that liberalism as the eighteenth century had known it required important modifications. The growth of a centralized and increasingly powerful state, with the parallel fading away of intermediate bodies and associations which might hinder its action—the whole process being backed up and justified by an appeal to the unlimited sovereignty of the people—this was a process of the dangers of which the eighteenth-century French liberals for the most part had had no inkling, and, indeed, which they in fact partially helped to bring about. By the first decades of the nineteenth century, however, it loomed as the central problem for liberalism, and the works of these three writers are in large measure a response to it.

The principles of traditionalist and theocratic conservatism, however, could not appeal to them (Acton, who provides a partial exception to this, sloughed off conservatism in his maturity, as we have seen). Rather, particularly in the case of Constant, they tended to see the ideas of a de Maistre or a Bonald as merely the mirror image of the revolutionary movement: both conservatives and left revolutionaries were united in proposing an authoritarian system of guidance and control over individuals; their differences had to do with *which* groups would exert control—whether the traditional elites of aristocracy and Church, or a new elite of revolutionary intellectuals. Moreover, the conservatives were blinded by their own interests in supposing that the danger of European society was to be found in anarchy and the disintegration of all structures of social and political authority. Constant and Tocqueville insisted (and John Stuart Mill was later to follow the latter on this) that, on the contrary, the more powerful current was towards a monstrously enlarged governmental apparatus untroubled by the slightest opposition and towards a social stagnation of the Chinese sort. (Acton, who strongly emphasized the role of the right of resistance to

---

[2] *Lectures on the French Revolution*, p. 19.

tyranny and of rebellion, may in this regard have also been thinking along these lines.)

In the face of the tendencies of modern society, the authors we have examined looked to religious faith to aid the cause of liberty. In the view of Constant and Tocqueville, the old quarrels of liberty and religion were obsolete; conditioned by historical circumstance, the older liberal mistrust of religion was, in the midst of an entirely new historical situation, misleading and dangerous. The break up of the alliance of Throne and Altar, which, if it had not been completed, could readily be foreseen, freed religious faith for political functions of a different sort. Given Constant's and Tocqueville's analyses of the dangers of the materialism and individualism that modern society will increasingly experience, and the threat these pose for liberal institutions, religious faith appeared as a welcome—indeed, an indispensable—ally.

Both French thinkers were, in addition, pluralists, and looked with favor on the flourishing of social institutions and authorities which might act as counterweights to the central government (and, with Tocqueville, to majority opinion as well), while fulfilling other important social functions. In an age in which the Church had been relegated to the ranks of a voluntary social institution, taking its place along with all others within the framework of an essentially secular state, there could be little danger in propping up its influence as much as possible in this way.

Acton, too, was a pluralist, but he was in a somewhat different position from the other two thinkers, to some extent precisely because of his own more serious religious commitment. As a Roman Catholic—and a Catholic under the pontificate of Pius IX—he could not so easily dismiss the threat which religion had traditionally posed for freedom. His own identification with the Catholic Church led him, on the one hand, to a preoccupation with the problem of religious persecution, which kept it, in his mature years, always before his mind; while at the same time, in view of the Syllabus of Errors and Vatican I, he had to take seriously the possibility of a future struggle between freedom and theology. Thus, ironically, of the three writers it is Acton who, in his later period, most sharply expresses his skepticism as to the alliance between liberty and religion.

In another important respect, also, Acton's views diverge from those of Constant and Tocqueville. While Constant is a product of the French Enlightenment in his hostility towards ecclesiastical religion, preferring the individual experience of "le sentiment religieux," and while Tocqueville does not make much of the distinction between feeling and form, in Acton's historical analysis it is precisely the most powerful and highly organized form of Western religion—the medieval papacy—which is most to be credited with aiding the cause of freedom. Acton's concentration on institutions rather than on psychological tendencies here is probably partially a reflection of the more sophisticated historiography of the nineteenth century. In addition, his analysis represents an advance in another sense: as we have seen, Acton makes it clear that the popes who tried to usurp royal and imperial power did not aim at liberal ends, and his use of the dialectical perspective appears to correspond more closely to the actual historical development than does Constant's residual "philosophical" condemnation of the role of all priestly religions.

The most fundamental similarity among the three thinkers has to do with the ethical coloration of their liberalism. For all of them, liberty was to be valued chiefly as a means to the end of human excellence, whether this is conceived of as consisting of perfect obedience to conscience, in such qualities as energy, passion and a taste for grandeur, or (as with Constant) in something of a combination of these. Accordingly, Constant and Acton condemned utilitarianism, the former devoting a good deal of effort to the enterprise. For both thinkers, egoism furnished an inadequate foundation for liberty. For Acton, this conclusion was tied to his basic philosophical *rationale* for rights, which were seen as proceeding from one's duties to one's neighbors. Constant's dread of the modern emphasis on egoism, on the other hand, stemmed from his view of the social conditions required for a liberal order. (Faguet, who states of Constant that "il a fait du libéralisme un égotisme intelligent,"[3] is greatly over simplifying Constant's complex thought in this area and, moreover, ignoring the clear meaning of various texts.)

Tocqueville followed Constant closely in his identification of egoistic individualism and the quest for personal enjoyment as a prime modern threat to freedom. (Indeed, the parallels between their thought in this whole area are so many—although unexplored by any scholar, to my knowledge—that a strong influence by Constant on Tocqueville must be presumed.) He appears at first to disagree with Constant in asserting that,

[3]Faguet, op. cit., p. 253.

given certain conditions, egoistic hedonism is an acceptable basis for ethics in the democratic age, *faute de mieux*. Ultimately, however, he finds that it is insufficient for the creation of the minimally necessary sort of human character, and must be supplemented by religion, by the cultivation of the sense of glory, etc. In fact, in the end, he grows silent concerning the potentiality even of religious faith to stem the modern attitude, and places his hopes rather in the practice of political democracy.

The recognition of the inadequacy of the ethical and metaphysical bases of eighteenth-century liberalism and the currents in nineteenth-century liberal thought that flowed from it, may be cited as the distinguishing mark of the three men whose ideas we have examined; of all of them, and not of Tocqueville alone, it may be said that "they were liberals of a new type."

Bibliography

Acton, Lord. *Essays on Freedom and Power*. Edited by Gertrude Himmelfarb. New York: Meridian, 1956.

———. *Lectures on the French Revolution*. New York: Noonday, 1959.

———. *Letters to Mary Gladstone*. Edited by Herbert Paul. London: Macmillan, 1905.

———. *Lord Acton and His Circle*. Edited by Abbot Gasquet. New York: Franklin, 1968.

———. *Selections from the Correspondence of the First Lord Acton*. Edited by J. N. Figgis and R. V. Laurence. London: Longmans, 1917.

Asse, Eugene. "Benjamin Constant et le Directoire." *Revue de la Revolution* 16 (August 1889): pp. 554–589.

Barker, Ernest. *Principles of Social and Political Theory*. Oxford: Oxford University, 1961.

Bastid, Paul. *Benjamin Constant et sa Doctrine*. Paris: Armand Collin, 1966.

Bauer, Juliette. *Lives of the Brothers Humboldt*. New York: Harper, 1853.

Bentham, Jeremy. *The Principles of Morals and Legislation*. New York: Hafner, 1965.

Brinton, Crane. *English Political Thought in the Nineteenth Century*. London: Hamish Hamilton, 1933.

Constant, Benjamin. *Cours de politique constitutionnelle*. Edited by Édouard Laboulaye. 2 vols. Paris: Guillaume, 1872.

———. *Œuvres*. Edited by Alfred Roulin. Paris: Pléiade, 1957.

———. *De la religion considéra ture dans sa source, ses formés et ses développement*. 5 vols.: Vol. 1. Paris: Leroux, 1824; Vol. 2. Paris: Bechet, 1825; Vol. 3. Paris: Bechet, 1827; Vols. 4 and 5. Paris: Pichon et Didier, 1931.

———. *Mélanges de littérature et de politique*. Paris: Pichon et Didier, 1829.

Coplestone, Frederick. *A History of Philosophy*. Vol. 6. London: Burns and Oates, 1960.

Dicey, A.V. *Lectures on the Relation between Law and Public Opinion in England during the Nineteenth Century*. London: Macmillan, 1905.

Drescher, Seymour. *Tocqueville and England*. Cambridge, Mass.: Harvard University, 1964.

Fabre-Luce, Alfred. *Benjamin Constant*. Paris: Fayard, 1939.

Faguet, Emile. *Politiques et moralistes du XIXe siècle*. Paris: Boiven, 1891.

Fasnacht, G.E. *Acton's Political Philosophy*. London: Hollis and Carter, 1952.

Fustel de Coulanges, Numa Denis. *The Ancient City*. No translator. Garden City, N.Y.: Anchor, 1956.

Gall, Lothar. *Benjamin Constant: Seine politische Ideenwelt und der deutsche Vormärz*. Wiesbaden: Steiner, 1963.

Geyl, Pieter. "The Idea of Liberty in History." In *Encounters in History*. New York: Meridian, 1961.

Hayek, F.A. *The Constitution of Liberty*. Chicago: University of Chicago, 1960.

———. "Individualism: True and False." In *Individualism and Economic Order*. Chicago: University of Chicago, 1948.

Himmelfarb, Gertrude. *Lord Acton*. Chicago: University of Chicago Press, 1962.

———. *Victorian Minds*. New York: Knopf, 1968.

Holdheim, William. *Benjamin Constant.* New York: Hillard, 1961.

Humboldt, Wilhelm von. *Werke.* Edited by Andreas Flitner and Klaus Giel. Vol. 1. Darmstadt: Wissenschaftliche Buchgesellschaft, 1960.

Hume, David. *On Religion.* Edited by Richard Wollheim. Cleveland, Ohio: Meridian, 1964.

Kochan, Lionel. *Acton on History.* London: Deutsch, 1954.

Laboulaye, Édouard. *L'état et ses limites.* Paris: Charpentier, 1865.

Lally, F. E. *As Lord Acton Says.* Newport, R.I.: Pioneer, 1942.

Lauris, Georges de. *Benjamin Constant et les droits individuels.* Paris: Rousseau, 1903.

Lieber, Francis. *On Civil Liberty and Self-Government.* Philadelphia: Lippincott, 1865.

Lively, Jack. *The Social and Political Thought of Alexis de Tocqueville.* Oxford: Clarendon, 1965.

Lukacs, John. "Comment on Tocqueville Article." *French Historical Studies* 2, no. 1 (1961): pp. 193–195.

MacDougall, Hugh A. *The Acton–Newman Relations.* New York: Fordham University, 1962.

MacIntyre, Alasdair. *A Short History of Ethics.* New York: Macmillan, 1966.

Mackintosh, James. *Memoirs.* Boston: Little, Brown, 1853.

Mathew, David. *Lord Acton and His Times.* University, Ala.: University of Alabama Press, 1968.

Maunier, René. "Benjamin Constant, historien des sociétés et des religions." *Revue de l'Histoire des Religions* 102 (1931): pp. 341–369.

May, Thomas Erskine. *Democracy in Europe.* New York: Widdleton, 1879.

Mayer, J.-P. *Prophet of the Mass Age: A Study of Alexis de Tocqueville.* London: Methuen, 1939.

Michel, Henri. *L'idée de l'état.* Paris: Hachette, 1896.

Mill, John Stuart. *Nature and Utility of Religion.* Indianapolis, Ind.: Bobbs-Merrill, 1958.

Montesquieu, Charles Secondât, Baron de. *De l'esprit des lois.* 2 vols. Paris: Garnier, 1961.

Moulin, Léo. "On the Evolution of the Meaning of the Word 'Individualism.'" *International Social Science Bulletin* 6 (1955): pp. 51–60.

Muntaneo, B. "Episodes kantiens en Suisse et en France." *Revue de Littérature Comparée* 17 (1935): pp. 171–247.

Nisbet, Robert A. *The Sociological Tradition.* New York: Basic Books, 1966.

Richter, Melvin. "Tocqueville and Algeria." *The Review of Politics* 25 (July 1963): pp. 277–299.

Rieff, Philip. *The Triumph of the Therapeutic.* New York: Harper and Row, 1966.

Rousseau, Jean-Jacques. *Du contrat social.* Paris: Garnier, n.d.

Ruggiero, Guido de. *The History of European Liberalism.* Boston: Beacon, 1959.

Saltet, Mathieu. *Benjamin Constant: Historien de la Religion.* Geneva: Société Générale d'Imprimerie, 1905.

Simpson, M. C. M., ed. *Correspondence and Conversations of Alexis de Tocqueville with Nassau Senior from 1834 to 1859.* 2 vols. London: King, 1872.

Talmon, J. L. *The Origins of Totalitarian Democracy.* London: Mercury, 1961.

Tocqueville, Alexis de. *Democracy in America.* Translated by Henry Reeve. 2 vols. New York: Vintage, 1954.

———. *"The European Revolution" and Correspondence with Gobineau.* Translated and edited by John Lukacs. Garden City, N.Y.: Anchor, 1959.

———. *Oeuvres completes.* Edited by J.-P. Mayer. Vol. 2, *L'ancien régime et la révolution.* 2 vols. Paris: Gallimard, 1952 and 1953; Vol 9, *Correspondance d'Alexis de Tocqueville et d'Arthur de Gobineau.* Paris: Gallimard, 1959.

———. *The Old Régime and the French Revolution.* Translated by Stuart Gilbert. Garden City, N.Y.: Anchor, 1959.

———. *Recollections.* Translated by Alexander Teixeira de Mattos. New York: Meridian, 1959.

Vinet, Alexander. *Outlines of Theology*. No translator. London: Strahen, 1866.

Weber, Max. *The Protestant Ethic and the Spirit of Capitalism*. New York: Scribner, 1958.

Woodward, E. L. "The Place of Lord Acton in the Liberal Movement of the Nineteenth Century." *Politica* 4 (August 1939): pp. 36–58.

Zetterbaum, Marvin. *Tocqueville and the Problem of Democracy*. Stanford, Cal.: Stanford University, 1967.

Index

About the Author

Ralph Raico is professor of European history at Buffalo State College and a Senior Fellow at the Ludwig von Mises Institute. He received his Ph.D. under F. A. Hayek and is a specialist on the history of liberty, the liberal tradition in Europe, and the relationship between war and the rise of the state. He is also the recipient of the 2000 Gary G. Schlarbaum Prize for Lifetime Achievement in the Cause of Liberty.